elementary school social studies:

A Guide to Current Research

Association for Supervision and Curriculum Development, NEA
1201 Sixteenth Street, N.W., Washington, D.C. 20036

elementary school social studies:

A Guide to Current Research

Maxine Dunfee
Professor of Education
Indiana University
Bloomington, Indiana

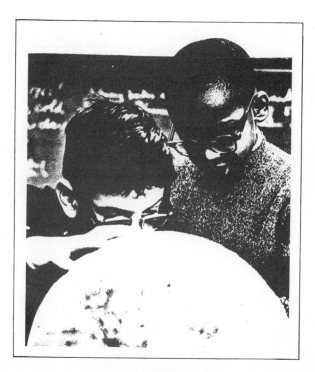

Price: $2.75
NEA Stock Number: 611-17384

The materials printed herein are the expressions of the
writers and not a statement of policy of the Association unless set
by resolution.

Library of Congress Catalog Card Number: 74-124604

Contents

Introduction

MORE than ten years ago the Association for Supervision and Curriculum Development planned to publish a survey of research in elementary social studies. When the publication became a reality, however, *social learning* rather than *social studies* was its focus.[1] The reason for this broader point of view? Limiting the booklet only to research in social studies education would have resulted in no publication at all, simply because there was not enough research in the field at that time to make the task worthwhile.

Now, on the threshold of a new decade, the situation is very different. Spurred by research in other aspects of the elementary curriculum and encouraged by the availability of grants for research purposes, social studies educators and social scientists have engaged in a host of projects, large and small, simple and complex. Nor is this research effort yet at an end.

While there is much still to be discovered about social studies in the elementary school, questions about goals and outcomes, curriculum concerns, the search for more knowledge about children, learning and inquiry, testing new materials and methods, construction of evaluation devices, and innovations in teacher education are all in the picture.

This booklet paints in abbreviated strokes various components of this scene. With no deliberate effort to evaluate methods or particular findings, the booklet clusters and reports summaries of available research in such a way as to make the study of particular concerns immediately possible. Graduate student members of a research seminar, Rutha Jack, Harry C. Dunn, James Coad, Edward Wright, Gene E. and Charlotte G. Daugherty, Imogene Ramsey, and Linda Olsen George, gave valuable assistance in locating sources and in preparing portions of the original draft.

May 1970   MAXINE DUNFEE

[1] Edna Ambrose and Alice Miel. *Children's Social Learning: Implications of Research and Expert Study.* Washington, D.C.: Association for Supervision and Curriculum Development, 1958.

vii

Acknowledgments

FINAL editing of the manuscript and production of this booklet were the responsibility of Robert R. Leeper, Associate Secretary and Editor, ASCD Publications. Technical production was handled by Mary Albert O'Neill, Lana G. Pipes, Nancy Olson, and Karen T. Brakke.

1. Goals for Social Studies

EFFORTS to survey current research are most relevant to social studies education when made within the framework of appropriate goals and objectives, just as any improvement of instruction which results from such a survey is most sound when it also takes place within this framework. To say that research in social studies for the elementary schools has gone forward without regard for objectives would, of course, be entirely inaccurate; on the other hand, research which has been directly concerned with identifying goals suitable to the demands of American society has been something less than concentrated or thorough. Nevertheless, when the educator views thoughtfully the research that has been undertaken, he can find some criteria or principles upon which to base his own goals for social studies instruction.

Goals for Education

At least two recent general statements of goals for American education have relevance to the problem of goal identification in the social studies. The 1960 report of the President's Commission on National Goals, *Goals for Americans* (128), is a good starting point, the result of searching thought on the part of a commission of distinguished and talented persons from varied segments of American life. The report brings together ideas and statements of beliefs pertinent to democracy, expressed in generalizations concerning the following: The Individual, Equality, The Democratic Process, Education, The Arts and Sciences, The Democratic Economy, Economic Growth, Technological Change, Agriculture, Living Conditions, Health and Welfare, Helping To Build an Open and Peaceful World, The Defense of the Free World, and Disarmament and the United Nations. Although these goals were not originally intended as guidelines for education, they certainly focus attention upon facets of American life which are the natural content of social studies. They are well worth consideration by curriculum builders.

1

Similarly the statement by another national group, The Central Policies Commission of the Educational Policies Commission, National Education Association, has authority and thoughtful scholarship to support it. *The Central Purpose of American Education* (92) strongly emphasizes the importance of developing powers of rational thought and the skills of inquiry to enable pupils to extend knowledge, to understand their world, and to solve its problems. The relationship of this statement to social studies instruction is at once obvious.

Content Goals for Social Studies

For a definitive statement of goals for social studies, teachers could do no better than to consult the National Council for the Social Studies, which represents professional social studies educators and in a sense speaks for them. A rather monumental effort was made by NCSS to identify major themes in content and to publish a report for the guidance of curriculum planners and teachers. It consists of a statement of 15 themes which define the content of the curriculum from kindergarten through grade 14. The themes suggested are the following (113: 11-52):

1. Recognition of the dignity and worth of the individual

2. The use of intelligence to improve human living

3. Recognition and understanding of world interdependence

4. The understanding of the major world cultures and culture areas

5. The intelligent uses of the natural environment

6. The vitalization of our democracy through an intelligent use of our public educational facilities

7. The intelligent acceptance, by individuals and groups, of responsibility for achieving democratic social action

8. Increasing the effectiveness of the family as a basic social institution

9. The effective development of moral and spiritual values

10. The intelligent and responsible sharing of power in order to attain justice

11. The intelligent utilization of scarce resources to attain the widest general well-being

12. Achievement of adequate horizons of loyalty

13. Cooperation in the interest of peace and welfare

14. Achieving a balance between social stability and social change

15. Widening and deepening the ability to live more richly.

In further search for guidelines to content, other studies have been designed to identify generalizations from the social sciences which could become integrative content goals for social studies. Hanna and Lee (148) report an extensive exploration into the social sciences to determine sources of content for social studies, a study involving in its various phases 21 doctoral candidates. These researchers produced more than 3,000 generalizations from history and the social sciences focused on basic human activities in expanding communities of men.

An effort in kind was undertaken by the California State Department of Education. The resulting list of generalizations for social studies, based on those identified by social scientists and agreed upon by educators, has been used widely as the basis for content in various curriculum developments around the country. The *California State Framework for the Social Studies* (264), which identifies 18 generalizations related to concepts of change, basic needs, environment, democracy, natural resources, interdependence, culture, and the like, gave great impetus to the movement away from facts and information toward concern for ideas of continuing applicability in human relationships. Many of the curriculum projects discussed in the next chapter also have made efforts to identify significant generalizations from the social sciences, notably the Greater Cleveland Social Science Program (94) and the Contra Costa Curriculum Project (318). Others, like the Anthropology Curriculum Project (16) and the Elkhart Indiana Experiment in Economic Education (292), have concentrated principally upon generalizations from a single social science discipline.

Similarly, the Wisconsin Social Studies Committee, with the help of research scholars from universities, identified basic conceptual ideas that comprise the central elements of history and each of the social sciences. *A Conceptual Framework for the Social Studies in Wisconsin Schools* (57) is a publication which consists of charts showing basic conceptual ideas in varying applications at each grade level, designed to bring continuity and growth in understanding as pupils progress through the elementary school. This is a useful guide for persons rethinking the social studies curriculum!

Some of the difficulties of securing agreement on generalizations from the social sciences to undergird social studies instruction may be inferred from a study by Kaltsounis (197). He asked 14 social scientists each to name five principles which would be most essential to social studies instruction. There was very little agreement among the social scientists and little awareness of the integrative nature of social studies. Most of the social scientists gave principles from their own disciplines, an indication that they need to know much more than they do about social studies in the school.

On the other hand, Wood (349) discovered that it was less difficult to find agreement on understandings from a single discipline. When he asked teachers, curriculum specialists, and sociologists to rate the importance of 182 sociological understandings, he found that teachers and curriculum workers agreed fairly well and that sociologists were able to come to some agreement on ideas basic to a knowledge of sociology.

Determining specific concepts and understandings related to the study of a specific country poses similar problems for curriculum workers. DeBoer (78) developed, for a study of Alaska, a technique for selecting and validating important concepts, a process which can be applied to other geographic areas chosen for study. She found that concepts from anthropology, geography, and economics were judged to be more useful than those from other social sciences and from the arts.

The Curriculum Center in the Social Studies at Syracuse University (257), a project sponsored by the Cooperative Research Branch of the U.S. Department of Health, Education, and Welfare, has identified three types of concepts: substantive concepts, value concepts, and concepts of methods. While the project does not attempt an all-inclusive list of concepts, it develops a number of very important ones that should be attended to as the child moves through school.

The substantive concepts which contribute to the selection of appropriate content in social studies are these: Sovereignty of the Nation-State in the Community of Nations; Conflict—Its Origin, Expression, and Resolution; The Industrialization-Urbanization Syndrome; Secularization; Compromise and Adjustment; Comparative Advantage; Power: Morality and Choice; Scarcity: Input and Output; Saving; The Modified Market Economy; Habitat and Its Significance; Culture; Institution; Social Control; Social Change; and Interaction. From these concepts are to be derived generalizations which state some relationship between or among the concepts.

Taba (319: 7-8), through the Contra Costa Curriculum Project, focused on basic knowledge as the first category of objectives, breaking this objective down into three additional levels: "Basic concepts are high level abstractions expressed in verbal cues. . . . Main ideas represent important generalizations. . . . Specific facts serve to develop the main ideas." To these knowledge objectives, of course, Taba added others which will be mentioned later.

Attitudes and Values as Goals of Social Studies

Attitudes, beliefs, and values are an important category of goals for social studies instruction, for they represent the keys to ways in which members of a society react and behave. While there has been some research to determine the attitudes and values held by elementary school children and teachers, there has been little attempt to determine what those attitudes and beliefs should be, at least beyond the philosophical level.

Again, however, the National Council for the Social Studies (244: 317) has developed subjectively a list of those beliefs it considers essential to the democratic way of life, a list for which there seems to be considerable support. This list includes beliefs in individual worth, equality of rights and liberties, equality of opportunity for self-development, group rights, the high priority of the common good, freedom of inquiry and expression, willingness to act on the basis of reasoned conclusion, government based on law, ability of people to govern themselves, freedom of economic competition consistent with general welfare, the values of both competition and cooperation, separation of church and state, maximum individual freedom under law, peaceful means of solving international problems, devotion to the heritage of the past, and commitment to perpetuate ideals of American life.

Another helpful delineation at the level of the affective domain is that by Krathwohl, Bloom, and Masia (204). While their taxonomy is not specifically directed toward social studies, the relationship of each level of objective to the development of attitudes, beliefs, and values in social studies is quite clear. The increasingly complex objectives—receiving, responding, valuing, organization, and characterization by a value or value complex—take the child from mere sensitivity to the existence of certain phenomena or stimuli to the very high-level state at which he has a code of behavior by which to guide his life. Surely such concerns are at the heart of social studies.

Value concepts were also included in the work of the Curriculum Center in the Social Studies at Syracuse University (257), concepts that are deeply enmeshed in the attitudes, opinions, and behaviors which citizens exhibit. The value concepts selected for particular attention in this study were these: the dignity of man, empathy, loyalty, government by consent of the governed, and freedom and equality. The study of values directed by Scriven (291) for the Social Science Education Consortium, however, led him to conclude that "equality of rights" is the only value that can be given even temporarily the status of an ultimate value.

Taba (319) interpreted this category of objectives as attitudes, feeling, and sensitivities: identification with people of various cultures, security that helps a person to be comfortable while being different, open-mindedness toward the opinions and behavior of others, acceptance of changes and adjustments to them, tolerance for the uncertain and the ambiguous, and response to human values and democratic ideals.

Behaviors and Process
as Goals of Social Studies

Ultimately the democratic society is most concerned with the reactions and behaviors of its citizens, for what they do fashions life for the future. Concepts and generalizations, and the attitudes and values such knowledges generate, are but the preparation for behaviors and skills which are to be exhibited in the everyday life of citizens. Social studies instruction cannot stop with development of only knowledge and attitudes; the conversion of these into action must be given serious attention.

Such behaviors and skills fall into two categories—habits of searching and thinking, and actions taken as a result of knowledge gained. The National Council for the Social Studies (244: 316) has listed the behavioral patterns which are deemed essential for the continued growth of democratic society:

1. Keeping well informed on issues which affect society, and relating principles and knowledge derived from the social sciences to the study of contemporary problems

2. Using democratic means in seeking agreement, reaching solutions, and taking group action on social problems

3. Assuming individual responsibility for carrying out group decisions and accepting the consequences of group action

4. Defending constitutional rights and freedoms for oneself and others

5. Respecting and complying with the law, regardless of personal feelings, and using legal means to change laws deemed inimical or invalid

6. Supporting persons and organizations working to improve society by desirable action

7. Scrutinizing the actions of public officials

8. Participating in elections at local, state, and national levels, and preparing oneself for intelligent voting in these elections

9. Opposing special privilege whenever it is incompatible with general welfare

10. Being prepared and willing to render public service and to give full-time service in emergencies

11. Engaging in continual reexamination of one's personal values as the value system of the nation.

In addition, the National Council for the Social Studies (244: 318, 327) has identified abilities and skills needed by pupils and adults for effective behavior—"skills centering on ways and means of handling social studies materials, skills of reflective thinking as applied to social studies problems, and skills in effective group participation." Detailed components of these skills also are specified.

The Curriculum Center in the Social Studies at Syracuse University (257) has identified such skills as concepts of method in a broad sense—historical method and points of view, the geographical approach, and causation—and as techniques—observation, classification, and measurement; analysis and synthesis; objectivity; skepticism; and interpretation. Essentially, these are components of the decision-making process.

Cognitive behaviors have received the closest scrutiny in recent studies and projects. The research project directed by Taba (319) places special emphasis upon thinking as one of its categories of objectives. The model curriculum developed in the project has attempted to break down the thinking act into three levels or sub-objectives: concept formation, resulting from the interrelating and organization of data; development of generalizations, representing the ways in which pupils interpret data and make inferences from them; and application of principles, representing the ways in which pupils apply to new situations what they have learned and make predictions of outcomes.

Closely related to such identification is the taxonomy of educational objectives by Bloom (28). His analysis of the hierarchy of skills in the cognitive domain—knowledge, comprehension, application, analysis, synthesis, and evaluation (with their clarifying sub-skills)—has been extremely useful in calling attention to the importance of rational power as an objective of social studies. Sanders (279) has made a useful "translation" of the taxonomy for teachers of social studies.

The emphasis upon process goals has been gaining steadily in recent months, shifting somewhat from the earlier stress, at the beginning of the decade, upon concepts and generalizations as components of the structure of social studies. One evidence of this interesting change is a recent publication of the California State Department of Education (309). Feeling that the needs of society today demand that pupils go beyond knowledge of the world as it is, or attention to its current social problems, the Social Sciences Study Committee has placed emphasis upon the mastery of the process of inquiry by which pupils may study human relationships.

This new proposal lists ten outcomes deemed desirable for all pupils. It includes the ability to do the following (309: 3):

1. Define issues, problems, and topics of study clearly, giving attention to values and other affective elements as well as to concepts and other cognitive elements

2. Select and use appropriate modes of inquiry in terms of the problem or topic under study

3. Select and use appropriate processes of inquiry in light of the mode of inquiry that is being used at a given time

4. Interpret data meaningfully, assess the accuracy of information, and communicate ideas effectively

5. Use concepts as tools to analyze problems, guide observation, make comparisons, classify data, interpret findings, and communicate ideas

6. Contrast or compare events and activities as appropriate to explore identities, similarities, and differences

7. Analyze rights, freedoms, and responsibilities in the context of relevant values and underlying conditions

8. Propose and evaluate solutions to problems in terms of consequence-analysis based on a priority of values

9. Make and test hypotheses and generalizations, taking account of relevant information and avoiding generalizations

10. Express and demonstrate ways in which fundamental values are a part of our American heritage.

Citizenship as a Goal of Social Studies

The goal of citizenship is of overriding importance in education and particularly in social studies. It has been the continuing component of almost every statement of social studies objectives. To identify the specifics of this goal was the task undertaken in 1965 by the Civic Education Project (272), sponsored by the National Council for the Social Studies. Members of the commission were asked to visit secondary schools of the nation to ask, "What is a good citizen?" Their conclusions are of importance to every elementary teacher as well (272: 415-19).

Goal 1. A citizen who believes in *both* liberty of the individual and equality of rights for all, as provided by the Constitution of the United States.

Goal 2. A citizen who recognizes that we live in an "open-end" world, and is receptive to new facts, new ideas, and new processes of living.

Goal 3. A citizen who makes value judgments that enable him to function constructively in a changing world.

Goal 4. A citizen who accepts the responsibility to participate in decision making by informing his representatives, experts, and specialists of his reactions to alternative public policies.

Goal 5. A citizen who develops skills and acquires knowledge to assist in the solution of political, economic, social, and cultural problems of his time.

Goal 6. A citizen who takes pride in the achievements of the United States, and at the same time appreciates the contributions to civilization of other peoples throughout the world.

Goal 7. A citizen who remains constantly aware of the tremendous effects of scientific discoveries on American and world civilizations, and works for their use in the quest for improved living for all mankind.

Goal 8. A citizen who realizes the importance of economic security and economic opportunity in the lives of all men, and concerns himself with strengthening both.

Goal 9. A citizen who uses the creative arts to sensitize himself to human experience and to develop the uniqueness of his personality.

Goal 10. A citizen who has compassion for other human beings, and is sensitive to their needs, feelings, and aspirations.

Goal 11. A citizen who understands that the continuation of human existence depends upon the reduction of national rivalries, and works for international cooperation and order.

Goal 12. A citizen who develops a set of principles consistent with his democratic heritage, and applies them conscientiously in his daily life.

A National View of Goals for Social Studies

Looking at the objectives for national assessment in social studies may be a useful way to bring to a close a survey of research concerned with goals. The plan for national assessment of attainment in the major fields of study in the public schools proposes to gather evidence on achievement at selected levels of maturity, in the various regions of the country, and from representative socioeconomic levels. Objectives for both citizenship and social studies were carefully selected by panels of scholars, teachers, and curriculum specialists, with importance of the objective to society as the agreed-upon criterion. Citizenship goals and social studies goals were separated because it became clear to the panel members that many areas of study contribute to the former and that these goals could not be included solely in social studies.

Campbell and Nichols (46) report the techniques for identifying the goals for citizenship and include some examples. Kurfman (206: 210-11) lists the five major objectives on which consensus was reached for social studies.

1. Within the limits of his maturity, a person competent in the area of social studies uses analytic, scientific procedures effectively. He identifies and defines problems and issues; he obtains information from a variety of sources; he formulates stable generalizations and hypotheses; he distinguishes relevant from irrelevant information and reliable from unreliable sources; and he detects logical errors and unstated assumptions.

2. A person competent in the area of social studies has knowledge relevant to the major ideas and concerns of social scientists. For example, he understands some of the major characteristics of economic systems, especially the American economic system. He understands something about spatial distributions and man's interaction with the physical environment.

3. He has a reasonable commitment to the values that sustain a free society. Examples of sub-objectives: He is committed to the fundamental worth of the individual—to the freedoms of the First Amend-

ment—to the Rule of Law—and to open opportunity for advancement. He is willing to act for the general interest and to participate in decision making when these decisions are relevant to his life.

4. He has curiosity about human affairs. Sub-objectives: He raises questions and seeks answers; he is open to new information and ideas; he tries to understand why other people think and act as they do.

5. He is sensitive to creative-intuitive methods of explaining the human condition. Sub-objectives: He reads history, philosophy, and fiction; he recognizes the role of creative-intuitive methods in scientific inquiry; he distinguishes personalized explanations of human affairs from scientific-objective explanations.

This statement of objectives assembled in concise and clear-cut fashion is representative of the content-affective-behavior and process goals described in this chapter. Knowledge on the national level of how well these goals are being attained would seem to be of real value in planning and improving the social studies curriculum. Many of the new developments reported in the following chapter reflect and reinforce these concerns.

2. The Social Studies Curriculum

BECAUSE of the breadth of its content and its changing nature, the social studies curriculum has been in a state of continual uncertainty almost from its earliest induction into the elementary school. Primarily existing at first as geography and history, it went through a series of changes—correlation, fusion, social learning—without becoming clearly defined in objective, content, or method.

Furthermore, having come into status as a curriculum area somewhat later than reading, writing, and mathematics, the social studies field frequently has been put aside in favor of skill development or entirely neglected simply because of its undefined nature. More recently, intense interest in the development of science in the elementary school has influenced further the time available for social studies.

Of course, this is not to say that no attention at all was given to the social studies curriculum prior to the present decade, the period of its greatest focus. Quite to the contrary. But these efforts were generally on the theoretical level and were not widely implemented in practice. While many forward-looking schools could be identified with one or more of the emerging trends, by and large the geography and history textbooks dominated the scene; and instruction was circumscribed by the content and method suggested by their authors.

Early Curriculum Efforts

At the risk of being too brief, it may be well here to call attention to a few of the breakthrough points in the development of the social studies curriculum in order to provide some historical background against which the points of view of current curriculum development projects and research efforts may be considered.

One of the ideas which pierced some holes in the shield of the textbook-centered, separate-subjects approach to social studies was the proposal which focused social studies instruction upon the com-

12

mon basic activities in which human beings engage as they go about the business of daily living—past, present, and future. The first to publish a curriculum based on social functions was the state of Virginia (59). In this course of study the school day was organized around problems of home life, community living, adaptation to environment, inventions and discoveries, and machine production; and pupils became actively involved in solving these problems. The integrative "unit of work" took form in this course of study.

The Virginia course of study served as a model for developing other curriculum plans, embodying both the social-functions idea and the widening-horizons approach to sequence, the latter being based on the assumption that children work best with the known environment when they are young and progressively become able to handle content from increasingly more remote locales. Textbooks, too, took up this widening-horizons (or expanding-environment) concept, which has persisted strongly to the present.

At this point it may be well to note that there are many critics of the widening-horizons concept, among them Smith and Cardinell (307), whose research indicated that children have interests that go beyond their immediate environment, and that television has a great influence on children's informational background and concerns. On the other hand, Hanna (147) has extended the widening-horizons idea—the expanding communities of men—superimposing upon it basic human activities which are the center of attention of people in all environments. Theoretically, then, Hanna sees these basic human activities as the concepts which become increasingly sharply defined as pupils explore the wider communities in which people live.

An even more comprehensive design for an interactive, integrative curriculum than that proposed in the Virginia Course of Study was the proposal by Stratemeyer and others (316), in which the program of the school was organized around "persistent life situations" children face as they grow to maturity. The comprehensive plan cut across the entire school day and provided for functional development of both content and skills. While not widely implemented in many schools, the provocative design had a subtle influence on curriculum planners and continues to be relevant to their deliberations.

A valuable perspective on the whole of social studies curriculum development may be secured through a study by Leef (214), who explored at intervals of 20 years the relationship between the social forces of each period and the social studies curriculum. She discovered that social forces—political, social, and economic—had indeed been reflected in social studies for the elementary school, but that in general these forces had not directed attention to any degree to the need for critical appraisal of the social order. The investigator did, however, find that the curriculum had become more and more closely related to real-life concerns of the learners.

In spite of these influences, however, before the decade of the sixties, the social studies curriculum was largely characterized by emphasis upon textbook content, concern for geography and history to the exclusion of other social sciences, expository methods based on recall and reproduction of information, survey rather than depth studies, and little pupil involvement either in planning or experiencing. There has been until recently little evidence to refute social studies critic Mayer (225: 222), whose critical survey produced evidence that facts and where to find them were largely the focus of social studies with little attendant concern for interpreting the facts and drawing conclusions from them.

New Developments in Social Studies

Fortunately, the curriculum improvement focus which in a sense has revolutionized instruction in both science and mathematics has in the past few years been trained upon social studies, bringing to life this area of the curriculum and influencing its status considerably. A great number of curriculum projects are identifying concepts and generalizations, developing scope and sequence proposals, probing in depth particular aspects of a social science, and producing materials.

The formal development projects have a variety of sponsors. One of the most extensive undertakings is Project Social Studies, supported by the Cooperative Research Branch of the U.S. Department of Health, Education, and Welfare (81; 101; 305). Since 1963, programs supported under this project have been under development with one or more of these ideas as point of focus—overcoming lag between research and practice, identifying the structure of social science disciplines, developing methods of inductive teaching, emphasizing sequential learning, examining new content, producing materials for pupils and teachers, and evaluating the use of these products. Other projects with similar incentives are being financed and sponsored by the National Science Foundation, private philanthropic organizations, universities, and public school systems.

One group of projects, already mentioned in the preceding chapter, has concentrated on the identification of concepts, themes, or generalizations upon which curriculum in social studies may or should be based. A committee of the National Council for the Social Studies produced a scholarly but practically-implemented list of 15 basic themes for the guidance of curriculum planners (113). An equally influential contribution to curriculum development has been the list of high-order generalizations produced by the State Central Committee on Social Studies for use in designing social studies curriculum in the state of California. These generalizations developed cooperatively by educators and scholars from the various disciplines have been widely cited and very frequently used by various groups in curriculum planning (264).

Similarly, conceptual ideas basic to each of the social sciences and history were identified by the Wisconsin Social Studies Committee (57), providing a structure for curriculum development in Wisconsin and leading to preparation of courses of study, resource units, and teaching materials. A useful feature of this proposal is that major concepts for each discipline are listed in chart form, with suggested sub-concepts and sequence recommendations. The Curriculum Center in the Social Studies at Syracuse University has also been engaged in identifying concepts from the social sciences and allied disciplines appropriate for the elementary and secondary program in social studies, in examining useful workways for these disciplines, and in evaluating at three grade levels illustrative materials which translate the concepts and workways into classroom practice (97; 256; 257).

Several of the current development projects have been devoted to the designing of articulated social studies programs for elementary through secondary school; some of these are already being published for general use. One of the major reform projects is the Greater Cleveland Social Science Program (94), a curriculum designed for kindergarten through twelfth grade, one intended to produce a clear understanding of the nature of the free society and to develop generalizations from the social sciences in an integrated way. Of particular interest is the third-grade in-depth study of Cleveland—its problems, resources, functions, and relationships to state, nation, and the world. Materials for both teachers and pupils are a part of this effort.

The Social Studies Curriculum Development Center at the University of Minnesota also undertook the development of a new curriculum for grades 1-14, including teaching guides and resource units (342; 343). In general, the plan has abandoned the widening-horizons concept of sequence, while using topics close to pupils' lives as the take-off points for comparative studies which emphasize concepts from anthropology, sociology, and geography in the primary grades, with the addition of economics at fourth grade, and special attention to history and geography at fifth- and sixth-grade levels. Heavy emphasis upon the behavioral sciences appears throughout as a result of concern for behavioral goals in the affective domain.

Culture regions and civilizations provide the framework for an elementary through secondary school program begun in 1964 at Rhode Island College under a grant from the U.S. Office of Education and utilizing the Providence Public Schools as the locale (300). The Providence Social Studies Curriculum Study has prepared unit teaching guides for an integrated approach which reflects important ideas from various social sciences. Primary grades focus on sociological patterns of family and community; older pupils concentrate on the regional concept as illustrated by various areas of the world and by various civilizations.

The Contra Costa Curriculum Project, revised as the Taba Social Studies Curriculum (324), is another which has developed a comprehensive, sequential social studies program for the elementary schools. Based on Taba's model for development of cognitive processes (110; 319; 320; 321), the program is designed to develop basic knowledge, critical thinking, attitudes, and skills of search and group work. Basic concepts serve as threads which run throughout the sequence; main ideas or generalizations serve as unit organizers; experiences are planned to develop inductive thinking. Content follows somewhat the widening-horizons approach, with special concern for California and its cultural heritage at the fourth-grade level. Taba's close association with development of the curriculum guides and the in-service education of the teachers has made the project a working model of her ideas about teaching social studies.

Some of the projects which have stirred the most comment and criticism, however, are those which concentrate more or less upon a single discipline. Such a controversial project is the one directed by Educational Services Incorporated (now Education Development Center) under the aegis of Jerome Bruner. In "Man: A Course of Study" (37), Bruner has implemented his ideas about teaching the structure of a discipline—in this case, largely anthropology. Through content seemingly far removed from that which most teachers consider appropriate for elementary children, Bruner and his associates have sought to develop some basic principles about the humanness of man, how he came to be that way, and how he can become more so. Four units—language, tools, social organizations, and child rearing—serve as models rather than as a complete curriculum. Methods emphasize inductive learning facilitated by special materials, games, films, and models. Typical of the criticism which this project has stimulated is that of Krug (205), who questions Bruner's preoccupation with structure, with anthropology to the exclusion of history and other social sciences, with overgeneralized objectives, and his neglect of significant problems in today's world.

Probably equally controversial is the Anthropology Curriculum Project at the University of Georgia (16; 266). The project provides materials in two cycles, one for primary and one for intermediate, the first emphasizing the concept of culture and the techniques of the anthropologist through study of primitive peoples, and the second replicating and reinforcing concepts introduced earlier. Through rather didactic methods of teaching, the pupils are introduced to many anthropological terms which are subsequently explained and illustrated through project-produced materials. This process is thought to result in a clarification of the structure of the discipline along the lines of Bruner's ideas, though the elements of inductive learning and teaching which are part of his philosophy seem to be much less prominent.

The Michigan Elementary Social Science Education Project directs its attention particularly to sociology and includes psychology and social anthropology (109; 217; 218). It patterns its design after current programs in the physical sciences, using a laboratory approach to a study of human behavior and emphasizing methods of inquiry. Six units—Friendliness, Unfriendliness; People and Groups Different from Ourselves; Getting Work Done Alone and in Groups; Social Influence; Decision Making; and Personal and Group Development—point up the uniqueness of its plan.

Projects in economics have had their share of the research spotlight, most notable among them being the Elkhart Indiana Experiment in Economic Education at Purdue University (292). Senesh (294), the director of the project, has identified the characteristics of the program—social-reality oriented, problem oriented, structure oriented, interdisciplinary, K-12 oriented, and space oriented (that is, related to earth). The program itself is built on five ideas basic to the structure of economics—scarcity, specialization, interdependence, market, and public policy. The curriculum, which is now available from commercial sources, includes teacher guides and pupil materials, films, and recordings (293).

In the area of economics education there are also materials developed by the Industrial Relations Center of the University of Chicago for grades four, five, and six (259). The objective of the project is to help elementary pupils develop concepts of consumption and production and the relationships between them. A unique feature of the sixth-grade program is a simulation entitled *Market* in which pupils buy and sell foods in grocery stores, taking the roles of consumers and retailers.

Such developments as these have stirred rather widespread interest in the status of instruction in economics. Brown (35) studied Louisiana public schools, for example, discovering that economic education was being given some attention and approval in many schools. Systems associated with programs developed by the Joint Council on Economic Education were more extensively involved in such instruction than schools on their own.

History in grades five, eight, and eleven is the concern of the Social Studies Curriculum Study Center at Northwestern University (211; 212). Integration of concepts from the social sciences with the study of American history was a basic guideline directed toward the elimination of repetition and overlap among the grades in which American history is taught. Beyond this one effort, there seems to be little interest in curriculum development stressing history at the elementary level.

Geography has come in for some measure of attention in the current social studies improvement effort. Bemis (22) surveyed all state departments of education and school systems in all cities over 100,000 population to determine the status of geography in the public schools. He found no one pattern of social studies organization and, beyond the third grade, little agreement as to what it should be. An integrated program of human and regional geography seemed to be supported by the data. Rice (265) gathered survey data which seemed to imply that there was lack of recognition of geography as a scholarly discipline and a decline in specific geographic instruction in the elementary school. On the other hand, in his survey of intermediate grades in Iowa, Minnesota, and South Dakota, Veltkamp (333) found considerable concern for geographic education but little evidence that teachers understood its objectives or were well-prepared to teach the subject.

Lee and Stampfer (213), drawing upon data from two investigations conducted under Project Social Studies at Northwestern University, concluded that a lengthened period of geographic instruction—from primary grades on—was essential to the maintenance of geographic skills. Also interested in geographic skills and understandings, Davies (72) used research methodology to develop a program of map skills and understandings for the intermediate grades and to determine its content by logical analysis. The product of his effort includes a developmental sequence of learning experiences for each of nine basic human activities, the whole designed to teach pupils to use maps as geographic tools.

At the University of California at Los Angeles, Crabtree (62; 63) has directed a project in geography for primary grades, a program based on the concept of areal association, and has developed strategies and instructional materials suitable for young children. The content consists of problematic situations involving events in which human behavior has been shaped by geographic forces. In another study Henzl (157) has been applying to structural ideas in geography a curriculum spiraling technique with special emphasis upon discovery learning.

Some recent curriculum efforts have been concerned with the political socialization of children. At present there seems to be interest in determining where pupils are in relation to political attitudes and interests. Jaros and others (182) found an unusually strong association between low socioeconomic status and negative political attitudes among the children of Appalachia as compared with most children in the United States.

Greenstein's (141) study bore similar fruit, showing that lower-status children felt that they had no part to play in political life of the world, no influence, and no way to cope with things as they are. On the other hand, he found that, generally speaking, children had rather supportive attitudes toward government and its leaders, were limited in political knowledge, and were not political radicals. Hess, Easton, and others (43; 163; 164; 165) conducted a study of 12,000 elementary school children from grades one through eight, a study which has produced evidence to show that the years between three and thirteen seem to be the important years in the formation of political attitudes and readiness for citizenship.

Arnoff (8) describes the Springfield Study in which seven elementary schools were selected as the sample from which pupils in grades two, three, and four were to study a unit on government. The concepts developed in the unit involved many terms, relationships, and topics not usually introduced in the elementary school curriculum—*law, trial, property tax, subpoena, campaign,* and the like. The study produced evidence that pupils were able to understand concepts of government at the local, state, and national levels and were able to deal with much more complex concepts than educators had assumed possible.

Related to the political socialization of children and youth is the study of controversial issues, although unfortunately research seems almost nonexistent, except for the work of McAulay (226). He asked 648 elementary school teachers of one Eastern state whether or not they used controversial issues in their social studies programs. Five hundred nineteen replied that they did not discuss controversial issues in their classrooms. Teachers of the primary grades listed divorce, separation of parents, religious practices, unacceptable personal and living habits, sex play, and racial characteristics as types of controversial issues which might be pertinent to the lives of their pupils. Intermediate grade teachers listed such topics as religion, communism, sex, industrial problems, political issues, world events (such as Castro in Cuba), class distinctions, racial characteristics, and right-wing groups. The study raises some serious questions about the relevance of the social studies curriculum when such issues are ignored.

An interesting study by Merritt (231) attempted to discover the kinds of materials about broad social conflicts which can be understood by sixth-grade pupils. Situations involving such pupils in social conflicts were fictionalized and presented to the subjects of the study, who read the stories and responded to a test of comprehension. The results showed that children at this level were able to take initial steps in understanding the nature of social conflicts, and on the basis of the findings the investigator recommended that such study should begin at an "early and impressionable age."

The development of intercultural and international understanding has been a feature of many of the integrative curricula discussed in this chapter and of particular focus in those in the area of anthropology. Additionally, there have been some particular efforts devoted to this very important matter. The Glens Falls Project (220), sponsored by the National Council for the Social Studies, was built on the belief that the study of world affairs is appropriate at every grade level and in every aspect of curriculum. The program was designed to help each pupil develop an increasing understanding of other peoples, a growing appreciation of other cultures, attitudes of respect for others, a sense of responsibility as to one's role in a world of nations, and an awareness of the realities of international problems. The project was characterized by total community commitment. On the whole it is quite reminiscent of a much earlier program—the Springfield Plan (53).

A research study by Lambert and Klineberg (207) offers striking evidence of the views children hold of their own and of foreign people and implies that early attention to the development of appropriate world views and attitudes is essential to intercultural and international understanding. That some progress has been made was evidenced in a study by Ahmed (4), whose analysis of social studies curriculum materials used before 1945 and after 1955 in 12 representative school systems revealed a definite trend toward influencing pupils in the direction of world citizenship.

Presently social studies educators are being faced with new concerns posed by proposals for "black studies," "black curriculum," and "black history." These proposals seek to provide for black children, and white children as well, formerly neglected areas of content designed to emphasize the role of blacks in the history and development of modern society. Such a proposal is the one by Smith (308), who, after studying American history books in relation to black-oriented content, designed for elementary school pupils 12 in-depth studies, drawn from the social sciences and with special emphasis upon the role of Afro-Americans.

The growing concern for such curriculum modification has been widened to include all minority groups who have been demeaned and disowned by the society, and there is evidence of positive curriculum effort to implement the discussion that is going on. A number of new programs are emphasizing acculturation and comparative studies; and there is a noticeable effort in the development of teaching materials about minority groups, particularly about black culture. A very useful example of the latter is the April 1969 issue of *Social Education* which contains a wealth of many kinds of teaching resources.

Much is currently being written to help educators understand children who have special needs; curriculum development no doubt will follow. Ponder (251), for example, has rather effectively identified common attitudes toward the disadvantaged which tend to affect adversely efforts to seek out workable teaching processes; he also has formulated some general principles in planning for these children. Maddox and Ross (224) studied the words and phrases which were thought to be disruptive of good relationships among the races and to have a depressing effect upon efforts to develop curriculum well suited to inner city boys and girls.

Several efforts more closely connected with curriculum may have helpful suggestions for others who are making plans. Edgar (91) reports the Project BRIDGE which attempted to orient middle-class college students to the problems of teaching in the ghetto. As an aspect of this project, the project directors involved their Negro junior high school subjects in a study of American history through biographies of famous black persons, thus helping the pupils learn successfully through improved self-image and better understanding of human relationships. Harney and Burgdorf (153) describe an experience in which campus school teachers at the University of Wisconsin used a current events clipping—a neighborhood disturbance between a youth gang and the police—to spur an examination of interaction as an approach to community problems.

Bryan (40) used a study of the out-of-school experiences of 22 deprived second-grade pupils to develop curriculum plans for them. Banks (19) reports an experience in which seventh-grade black pupils were confronted with a series of historical documents to stimulate problem-raising about their heritage.

A relevant project directed toward the development of curriculum suited to the needs of inner city children was undertaken at the Adams-Morgan Elementary School. Burnes and Hershberger (42) report the experiences of six graduate students who volunteered to undertake as a class assignment the planning of a social studies curriculum emphasizing inquiry as its major focus.

A three-year project in Wilmington, Delaware (66; 67), focused curriculum planning on human relationships as they surface in changing neighborhoods, segregation and integration, economic forces in the inner city, and population movements in the city. The resulting curriculum was made the core of the school's program at each level.

A great variety of materials, programs, and projects related to urban education have been sponsored by the U.S. Office of Education through the Great Cities Program for School Improvement, an organization of large cities whose purpose is to conduct studies of the problems peculiar to public education in the city environment. An extensive survey report of locally-developed products in this program (64) is evidence of the creative approach many groups are taking to reach inner city children, teachers, and parents with a view to making education a more integral part of the urban scene.

Trends and Appraisals

In addition to the curriculum developments described here, there are many others; local and state projects are increasing rapidly in number. Certainly the period of the 1960's has witnessed unprecedented activity in the social studies. The significance of these efforts remains to be seen; obviously their very diversity raises questions about their chances for survival or integration in the school program. The Social Science Education Consortium (238; 239) has been concerned with the exchange of ideas among social science curriculum project workers and has subsequently published a conference report summarizing such topics as the structure of knowledge, the question of values, and the processes of learning and their curriculum implications.

As the array of curriculum development projects is spread before the educator, several trends are clearly visible. Fraser (112) identifies the following:

1. The search for a conceptual framework
2. An increased emphasis on sequence
3. New views of readiness
4. The thrust of the behavioral sciences
5. Depth studies instead of surveys
6. A comprehensive world view
7. Instruction based on inquiry
8. Multi-media learning materials and procedures
9. A climate of experimentation and innovation
10. Social scientists and educators work together.

The great variety and diversity of programs being developed also point up the need for criteria by which these programs can be evaluated by interested educators who may be studying them as preparation for projects of their own or who are considering adaptations for use in their own schools. Jarolimek (178) proposes 12 guidelines which may be used in making decisions about the quality and appropriateness of any new program or practice.

1. Are the major purposes of the program clearly stated in terms of pupil behavior, realistically attainable, and consistent with the philosophy of a democratic society?

2. Is the program psychologically sound?

3. Does the program show evidence of providing for balance in its attention to cognitive, affective, and skills objectives?

4. Does the program provide for sequential and systematic development of concepts and skills that are believed to be important?

5. Are the criteria for the selection of substantive content clearly specified in the program?

6. Is the program of instruction relevant to the lives of the pupils?

7. Is the scope of the program realistic in terms of the contemporary world and the backgrounds of today's pupils?

8. Are the learning activities and instructional resources consistent with the stated purposes of the program?

9. Does the program provide adequately for differentiated instruction?

10. Is the program one that teachers will understand and be able to implement?

11. Are the curriculum documents sufficiently structured to provide the teacher with direction, yet flexible enough to allow individual teacher initiative and creativity?

12. Is it possible to evaluate the program in order to establish with some degree of confidence the extent to which major purposes have been achieved?

For a critical appraisal of particular national projects in social studies, readers may refer to the April 1970 issue of *Social Education,* designed to help teachers and curriculum specialists select for further study project materials which may seem relevant to local situations. Program developments are described in terms of rationale, continuity, and sequence; cognitive, affective, and psychomotor objectives; instructional materials and strategies; approaches to evaluation and in-service education; special needs, problems, or costs; and alternate uses for all or parts of the program.

3. Children and Social Studies

RESEARCHERS have been discovering more and more about the readiness of children to learn concepts and skills associated with social studies in the elementary classroom. Numerous and varied investigations conducted since 1960 have examined the knowledges, interests, skills, and attitudes children bring to social studies instruction.

Knowledge Prior to Instruction

Of particular interest to the teacher of social studies is the knowledge which pupils have prior to instruction, since such information is invaluable in planning for instruction to meet individual interests and needs. For example, Goldstein (133) found that first-grade pupils enter school with far more knowledge of land features than is usually expected. After working with 87 entering first-grade pupils in the identification of 23 landforms and waterforms, such as mountains, rivers, and lakes, he concluded that social studies programs should be revised to take into account pupils' higher level of information.

Lowry (221) conducted a survey of 287 second-grade children from three sections of the country to determine their knowledge before instruction. The pupils were interviewed individually and recorded on tape. She found that pupils were familiar with 85 percent of the 110 concepts found in their social studies text. Kaltsounis (196) found that third-grade pupils knew 37 percent of the social studies for their grade before instruction; and Penner (248), who studied the extent to which 491 fourth-grade pupils from four states were familiar at the beginning of the school year with geographical concepts usually taught in the fourth grade, obtained results that indicated that pupils knew almost half the concepts common to ten current textbook editions. These investigators all concluded that elementary school children possess a higher degree of knowledge of social studies information and concepts than is generally supposed.

On the other hand, Mugge (243) interpreted somewhat differently evidence derived from her study of pupils' knowledge prior to instruction. Her investigation was designed to ascertain what information second-grade children could be expected to have in social studies before topics were introduced for study. The children were asked to respond to a test of social studies information, another test dealing with content outside their environment, a questionnaire related to definitions, and one relating to experiences. The informational test questions were secured from seven textbooks and from recent social studies curriculum guides; the definition test required pupils to define some of the terms they had been asked to use in the information test.

The results indicated that pupils in general responded correctly to about one-third of the questions on the informational test and more than half the questions on definitions. There was a definite relationship between the variety of experiences the pupils had had and the scores they received. There were many misconceptions and gaps in learnings, which confirmed Mugge's belief that children do vary greatly in readiness for social studies, just as they vary in their experiential background. Mugge is of the opinion that evidence of pupils' acquisition of information may mislead the teacher to overlook their lack of ability to systematize, store, and use such information. A similar study (242) with first-grade pupils convinced Mugge that children at this level are ready to learn concepts, but only those that require a single criterion of classification.

In any case, it seems clear that today's children are often underestimated by their teachers, who may not be aware of the experiential background of their pupils. Certainly teachers nee to know more about the wide range of differences that exist in group.

In view of evidence that pupils bring considerable knowledg to their social studies classroom, is their interest in social studi high or low? To pursue this question, Herman (159; 160) used interest inventory in which pupils were asked to state their pref ence for typical activities in the elementary school subjects. M than 200 Pennsylvania fourth-, fifth-, and sixth-grade pupils sponded in such a way as to indicate social studies as one of least-liked school subjects. In a study by Curry (69) nearly 44,(0 fifth-grade pupils ranked social studies ninth in a list of nine sible subject choices. Green (138) sought to discover pupils' cific interests in social studies. In this study, intermediate pupils preferred sociology and liked economics least; primary pupils liked political science most and anthropology least; girls preferred sociology but disliked economics; boys chose geography as the favorite and anthropology as least favored.

Adams (1) created a situation in which fifth- and sixth-grade children were motivated to ask questions about social studies. While the average number of questions was 4.3, thirty-four percent of the pupils asked no questions at all. More questions came from girls than boys, from younger pupils than older ones, and from pupils with higher intelligence quotients and socioeconomic level. In general, pupils who asked questions appeared to have a positive attitude toward social studies; those who did not were negative in their reactions. Such findings as these open up the question of the relationship of pupil interests to ability to handle concepts drawn from the various social sciences and the relationship of interests and abilities to the degree of challenge social studies offer the child who brings considerable knowledge with him to the classroom.

Equally important is pupils' ability to formulate and to comprehend concepts basic to various aspects of social studies. Wann and others (336) studied children three to six years of age to determine what they could understand about their world. The method of study employed was that of action research designed to systematically study children's ability to understand. After two years of study on the problem-solving behavior of their subjects, the investigators concluded that children employed the essential process of concept formation in their efforts to seek more and more information and that they tried to relate and test one bit of information against another. Spodek (311), using the basic concepts of history and geography in dealing with the topic "New York as a Harbor," concluded that kindergarten children can begin to develop significant social science concepts by dealing with concrete objects, real or representational. They can deal with ideas over a long period of time and gather information in many ways. They can also transfer their understandings to new situations.

Field (102) purposed to develop a verbal-pictorial measuring instrument of 106 second-grade social studies concepts (selected from five recent textbooks) by which to determine if statistically significant differences in prior social studies knowledge might be due to scholastic aptitude, chronological age, grade level, or sex. In a study of 120 pupils selected from a population of 1,308, grade level proved to be the most highly significant variable, while sex was of no significance. On the other hand, Rogers and Layton (270), who gave to more than 100 first- and second-grade pupils seven tests related to four social studies topics, found that a substantial number of the children demonstrated an ability to conceptualize at the correct level, with no significant difference appearing between the two grade level groups except in the items related to transportation. Although it might be concluded that little or no growth occurred during the two-year period, the researcher felt that such a conclusion would be better based if the study had been a longitudinal one.

Sixth-grade pupils were subjects in an investigation by Schiele (282), who studied their ability to explain conceptions of common terms appearing in a sixth-grade textbook. Pupils tended to score higher on a multiple-choice test of understanding than they did when they were asked to define the same concepts with concrete objects. Children of higher intelligence had less need of concrete objects to express their ideas than pupils of lower intelligence.

Concepts of Time

Concepts of time have received particular attention from researchers interested in pupils' conceptual development. There is no doubt, of course, that the ability to conceptualize time and space relationships is important in social studies.

Although a survey by Dobbs (82) of the research and literature indicated that there are conflicting opinions in this area, some investigators are convinced that time and space concepts are too difficult for children before the intermediate and junior high school levels. However, Stephens (313) is one of several researchers who have found that planned instruction in time concepts results in successful learning by kindergarten pupils.

McAulay (229) conducted a study to determine what understandings second-grade children have of time relationships. He selected 165 pupils from suburban middle-class families in an industrial city, from lower-class families in a railroad industrial town, and from families in a professional college community. The children were asked questions which would reveal their understandings of time which are associated with self (Who do you think has lived longer, your mother or your grandmother?), with the immediate environment (Which will be here first, Christmas or Easter?), and with historical events (Who lived first, Washington or Lincoln?). Results indicated that social studies programs for second grade underestimate the child's understanding of time.

Although these pupils seemed to have little comprehension of continuity of time as it is related to self or to the immediate environment, they understood periods of time which were concerned with events rather than with persons and places; they associated persons from history with one another, and they retained some information about such persons and events.

A study to determine the differences among pupils in the interpretation of indefinite expressions of time commonly found in textbooks was conducted by Gill (125). He asked 254 college, high school, junior high school, and intermediate-grade pupils to respond to 18 indefinite expressions of time used in American history. He concluded that such expressions are loosely interpreted at all levels, that a time sense and maturity are closely related, and that vague expressions in textbooks should be replaced by more exact ones whenever possible.

Time relationship understandings were investigated in grades four through eight by Legere (215). He hypothesized that time relationship understanding is a tri-factored element—associative, spatial, and mathematical; that the elementary child displays parallel and interrelated growth during maturation; and that children display a higher degree of awareness of time than has been assumed generally. He concluded that children who enter fourth grade do display the tri-factored element, with the associative being the most difficult base to use and the mathematical the earliest. All three emerge as a separate ability when used in an interrelated way by the learner to deal with multi-faceted problems or concepts.

Fifth- and sixth-grade pupils were of interest to Chase (52), who gave them a test of four questions in which they were required to place five items in each question in chronological order. He concluded that there was a range of individual differences among these pupils, and that, although pupils at these grade levels may not be ready for instruction in time relationships, instruction need not be deferred for all pupils at this point in their education. On the other hand, Arnsdorf (10), determining the effect of organized instructional attempts to increase children's ability to understand time concepts as they are employed in social studies, concluded that children can profit from such instruction.

A review of the studies of time concepts seems to indicate that children may be able to understand time and chronology concepts at an earlier age than previously predicted and that many children are receptive to planned instruction in these relationships.

Map Skills and Concepts of Space

Because concepts of space and skills in using maps are essential to social studies instruction, it is understandable why researchers have been attracted to this concern. The numerous studies reported here embrace both pupils' abilities and their achievement as a result of specific instruction.

Disadvantaged kindergarten pupils were taught concepts related to ideas of the earth as a globe in a program developed by Portugaly (252). Although the number of subjects was limited, results of instruction indicated that pupils were gaining an understanding of the relationships of earth and sun and were developing skill in dealing with models. The study seems to lend support to increased emphasis upon globe concepts at an early school level.

Second-grade children were the subjects used by McAulay (227) in a study of map abilities. He explored with 214 middle-class pupils the ability to use maps to secure information, to transfer oral directions to the abstractions of a map, to make comparisons and judgments in simple map work, to understand an experience through a map medium, and to determine whether or not map understandings are more closely related to the child's immediate environment or to a removed environment. The results showed that the pupils could use maps to secure information not only about the local community but about other environments, could visualize different environmental situations, and could transfer directions to a map situation. Less mature pupils were more able when map experiences were linked with the reality of their experience.

Two studies of achievement are pertinent at this point. Rushdoony (274) used an experimental group of 129 third-grade pupils who were taught the map-reading skills usually recommended for grades four and five; 90 minutes of instruction weekly were given over a period of 15 weeks. Again results showed that the subjects were able to learn many of the skills normally taught at higher grade levels. Stampfer (312) used an instrument based on the Joyce Sequence of Map and Globe Skills in Elementary Schools to study the achievement of 600 fourth-, fifth-, and sixth-grade pupils. For 16 of the 30 map skill items there was no significant difference among the three grade levels, although a pattern of increasing levels of mastery had been anticipated.

Intermediate-grade pupils were also the subjects of a study by Carswell (49), who was interested in their ability to read map symbols, direction, scale, elevation, and grid systems, and in their ability to interpret information from maps. After instruction, Carswell used his Test of Topographic Map Skills to determine pupil achievement. The results provided evidence that fourth-, fifth-, and sixth-grade pupils were able to learn to use large-scale topographic maps and were able to retain this skill even after a period of time.

A search of the professional literature of geography and a critical analysis by Farrar (99) led to certain conclusions about the map skills and understandings of upper-grade elementary children. As a result of his study, he concluded that these children should be able to verbalize mapped relationships into common symbols, read and interpret various kinds of maps, and make simple large- and small-scale maps of an area. Movement and time relationships of sun and earth, computation and measurement of map projection grid systems, and compilation of statistics of man-land activities and their use for geographic interpretation all appeared to be within the capabilities of these older pupils. Zimmer (350) constructed and administered to upper-elementary pupils a diagnostic test of a variety of map skills applied to hypothetical maps. She found that certain errors persisted through the grades and that pupils had special difficulties in the use of scale and latitude. There was noticeable improvement, however, especially between grades five and six.

A study by Davis (75) related to geographic concepts but also to concepts of time and space. He subjected fourth-, fifth-, and sixth-grade pupils to planned instruction about time zones. All grade groups benefited, but sixth more than fifth and fifth more than fourth. He noted with satisfaction that pupils continued to gain in understanding even after the termination of instruction. He commented also about the probability that pupils may be able to profit from instruction about time zones earlier than previously thought.

Map reading and geographic understandings taught through the use of 13 projectuals were investigated by Arnsdorf (13). Twelve lessons of about one hour each, spread over a six-week period, were designed to develop an understanding of what each projectual included, how the characteristics were distributed throughout the country, and the relationship of each feature to other features. Boundaries, mountains, railways, manufacturing, mineral resources, physiographic regions, river systems, land use, growing seasons, precipitation, vegetation, and population were included in the overlays to be used with an outline map of the United States. Emphasis was placed especially upon the questions asked by the 234 fifth-grade children in the study. The researcher concluded that a program employing such overlays and encouraging pupils to raise questions and probe relationships promotes both interest in geography as a social science and growth in understanding of map relationships.

Schumacher (290), studying the understandings of fifth- and sixth-grade pupils about the surface features of the earth, discovered that these pupils found it difficult to understand surface terms in a written setting and that there were significant differences between the achievements of fifth- and sixth-grade pupils. Consequently, the year between these levels appears to be an important one in terms of achievement of understanding.

Several recent studies have been undertaken to determine the age levels at which various concepts or skills develop and their grade placement. For example, Towler and Nelson (328), after a study of children from each grade level in a Canadian school system, concluded that children do not develop a concept of scale before the age of ten or eleven, even though they are frequently presented with map situations which require such knowledge at an earlier age. Miller (235) asked elementary-school pupils to judge from what direction each of a series of pictures of a three-dimensional map had been taken. He found the ability to measure perspective to be well developed by age twelve, but that few children before first or second grade were able to coordinate perspectives.

Gengler (122), in order to discover whether or not boys and girls could identify common geographical terms on a map, tested approximately 200 sixth-grade pupils. Identifications on the map, supplemented at times with verbal definition, varied widely with the concept. He concluded that verbal capability and ability to identify on the map are separate skills for both boys and girls. Joyce (195) attempted to develop a scheme for grade placement of map and globe skills by submitting to consultants a list of skills extracted from professional materials in geography. As forecast by studies already reviewed here, the estimate of grade placement by consultants was conservative when compared to their placement in experimental programs of instruction.

These studies seem to indicate that the early introduction of map and globe concepts and skills is more feasible than generally supposed and that systematic instruction is preferable to casual or incidental treatment. However, more research is needed to deter mine when children can develop an understanding of these concepts and skills in order to provide a proper learning sequence for each child at just the right time.

Concepts from the Social Sciences

Studies of children's readiness, knowledge, or abilities in the social sciences and of their understanding of concepts other than time and space have added to the store of information about pupils' potential for growth in social studies.

Some investigators, for example, have expressed concern over the ability of elementary school pupils to develop and understand broad social concepts and generalizations. A study to investigate the dimensions of children's understanding of three social science generalizations was undertaken by Beaubier (20), who used 228 sixth-grade pupils divided into control and experimental groups. An effort was made to present materials of greater complexity to the experimental group. Evaluation of pretests and post-tests showed that experimental groups achieved greater understanding in all areas and that differences between experimental and control groups were greatest in economics and anthropology. This researcher also came to the conclusion that children can learn concepts of greater complexity than is typically expected of them.

Several researchers have looked at children's concepts of political science. The Estvans (95) concluded that boys and girls enter school with little concept of government and that, although their grasp of governmental processes increases by the sixth grade, ideas and attitudes about government are slow to appear and mature. They urge early identification of various stages in children's growth of concepts, attitudes, and skills related to government. Greenstein (141), as a result of his study of children in grades four through eight, came to the conclusion that children have a low-level awareness of the work of public officials. They tend to rate their roles as more important than the roles of doctors, teachers, or ministers. However, this positive evaluation of the public official decreases with the age of the pupils. Party choices, which are usually those of parents, show little understanding of party differences.

Easton and Hess (89; 164) studied 12,000 elementary school children from grades one to eight to discover their attitudes and awareness of their political world and to find out when political motivation becomes a reality. The evidence indicated that many values and attitudes toward the political world have become well-established in the elementary grades, and that the years between three and thirteen are the most crucial in the formation of political motivation. In these years, the researchers say, children are as ready as they will ever be to learn about good citizenship.

Jaros' (181) study of children's orientations toward the President confirms the idea that the early years in which certain socialization processes develop are perhaps more important than is formal instruction in civics at a somewhat later time. Easton and Dennis (88) report in great detail their findings related to children's images of government. In the cognitive domain young children saw government as personal in character with a few visible leaders; as children matured, government was differentiated from private life in its functions and group character. In the affective domain the child at first had simple notions of government embodied in a President; later the child acquired ideas of support for and sympathy with government, ideas which seemed national in scope. The authors emphasize the unifying effect such an image of government has in a system like that which exists in the United States.

Schnepf (286) chose to look at Negro children's knowledge of and attitudes toward the police, law, and freedom. Her subjects were chosen from segregated neighborhoods in grades two, four, six, and eight. She found that all grades held positive attitudes toward law but unfavorable attitudes toward police and freedom, negative feelings which intensified as pupils progressed through the elementary school. In view of pupils' attitudes toward authority figures, the study suggested the need for reevaluating early citizenship education.

Geography is well represented in recent studies of the various social sciences, perhaps because traditionally it has been accepted as a separate school subject and has not had to find its place in the elementary classroom. Sheridan (298; 299) measured first-grade children's awareness of 30 selected concepts of physical geography. He found that almost all had an awareness of most of the concepts, an awareness that extended beyond the immediate environment. He noted that the sources of pupils' awareness were likely to be direct contact, television, and parents.

Research by Wallace (335) tested the ability of culturally-advantaged primary school pupils to comprehend geographic concepts taught by three different approaches. An inductive approach emphasized guided discovery; a deductive approach, characterized as verbal reception, presented to the pupils knowledge to be learn and internalized; an intuitive approach was similar to the inductive except that fewer cues were provided and greater premium placed on insight—a "leaping ahead" phenomenon. Second- and third-grade pupils were successful with all three approaches, but for the group being tested the deductive approach seemed to be most appropriate.

Sixth-grade pupils were the subjects chosen by two other researchers. Brown (33) used a group of 487 Kansas pupils for the dual purpose of identifying principles of physical geography for instruction and ascertaining the knowledge of these principles possessed by pupils. The principles, chosen from the literature and validated by a panel of experts, were incorporated in a test to which the pupils responded. Brown concluded that the principles should be included in the curriculum but that current practice falls short of producing mastery of the principles.

Weber's (338) study indicated that sixth-grade pupils were unable to make predictions or draw inferences concerning the influence of the natural environment on man. He found the inference level of his subjects only slightly above the "specific without elaboration" level. He hypothesized that their lack of success may have been caused by inability to see and consider significant features, to discriminate, and to understand relationships among environmental features.

Belgum (21) successfully used geographic photographs to teach sixth-grade pupils skills in the identification and interpretation of physical and cultural features in the landscape. Using her Photograph Interpretation Test for three different types of photographs found in elementary social studies materials, she assessed pupils' ability to identify, interpret, and make synthesizing generalizations. Results indicated that intelligence was positively related to success in using geographic photographs.

In the other social sciences, studies have not as yet been numerous. History has not been widely represented except, of course, in the studies of chronology, already reviewed. Guzetta (144), however, did conduct a study of children's knowledge of historically important Americans whose names had been found common to 11 textbooks in social studies and whose importance was confirmed by a panel of experts. He found that children did possess knowledge of historical personages and events before formal instruction, which usually begins at about the fifth grade. However, the panel of experts pointed out that the textbook lists of names failed to include other than persons from the political realm; artists and scientists, for example, were not included.

In the field of economics, Larkins (208) undertook to assess the ability of first-grade pupils to achieve an understanding of the concepts developed in the materials prepared for the Elkhart Indiana Experiment in Economic Education. The investigator found that pupils had no difficulty with the learning and that both above-average and below-average pupils were challenged by the content. Spears (310) studied four first grades, one using the materials of the Elkhart Experiment, two using other planned programs of economic education, and one serving as a control group. All the experimental groups performed better than the control group, supporting further the hypothesis that young pupils can learn quite sophisticated concepts drawn from economics. Darrin (70), through a program emphasizing developmental learning, found that children in classes from kindergarten through the sixth grade could understand basic economic concepts, their success improving with grade level.

In a study with a somewhat similar purpose but in a different field, Potterfield (254) analyzed pupils' ability to learn anthropological content developed for fourth grade by the Anthropology Curriculum Project at the University of Georgia. The researcher in this case, however, was interested to know whether or not teaching style, grade level, sex, socioeconomic level, or achievement had any effect on pupils' ability to learn. He found no significant differences in the ability of pupils at various grade levels, though the experimental groups outperformed the control group. No differences were found for grade, sex, socioeconomic status, or achievement level. Furthermore, specialized training for the teacher did not appear to be essential.

Social Values and Attitudes

Another group of studies about children has explored various facets of the development of values and attitudes as they relate to self, to the immediate scene, and to other people. Of special interest has been the development of sensitivity and concern as studied by Rogers (269), who surveyed the research that has been done and posed a number of fascinating questions which could profitably occupy investigators in the future. Rogers and Long (271) sought the answer to one of these in their study of the development of social sensitivity in elementary school children.

They invited 188 second-, fourth-, and sixth-grade pupils to respond to a 27-item paired comparison based on a series of described situations. Pupils were asked to decide to whom they would contribute $10 in a specific need situation—to people near at home (local), to people at some distance (national), or to people far away (international). A week after the responses, pupils were asked to tell why they gave their money as they did—second graders orally, others in writing. Second-grade pupils generally chose to contribute to people far away, and the two older groups were even more prone to do so. In explaining their actions, pupils seemed to see their own country as rich and in little need of help; other lands they viewed as more likely to be poor. While the researchers were pleased with pupils' concern for others, they were disturbed by pupils' lack of knowledge of the needs of people in their own country.

Ruderman (273) asked 294 children of nine through twelve years to record their reaction to each of 29 drawn pictures of various family interactions, presented to them in multiple-choice form. The researcher found that in this group empathy tended to increase with age and without relationship to sex. Intelligence seemed related to empathy but more as it was evidenced in cognitive awareness of the social and emotional environment than in intelligence per se. Children from smaller families seemed more empathic than those from larger families, while the ordinal position of the child in the family seemed relevant also.

Another group of studies had as its purpose the testing of ideas of value clarification. Raths (262) tested the hypothesis that helping pupils clarify their values would increase their participation in the learning activities of the school. Pupils of grades five through eight in a campus laboratory school were the subjects; their teachers used the daily experiences of the curriculum to explore the matter of values. With such questions as "Are you glad you feel this way? Is this something you prize? What are some things good about it?" teachers helped pupils probe their feelings and motives. Free writing, discussion of incidents, and role playing were used to provide evidence of possible changes in pupil behavior. The emphasis upon value clarification did in fact result in increased involvement in learning activities for all but 12 of the 100 pupils in the study.

Raths (263) tested the value of the clarification process in improving the achievement of underachievers at the high school level and found that the process affected positively the cognitive development of these pupils. Other studies to test these ideas have also been successfully carried out by Klevan (202), Jonas (189), and Gagnon (118).

A study of somewhat different nature but related to attitudes and values was conducted by Bottorff (30), who investigated the attitudes of white and black children of lower economic levels and middle-class white pupils toward certain key social studies words. Each child was given a booklet containing the words, one to a page. The child was directed to record his reaction to the word—sometimes "like" or "dislike" and sometimes the meaning—in the booklet. The responses were then identified as negative, positive, or neutral. The middle-class children responded more positively to the words than did lower-class groups. The word "black" was responded to negatively by both groups of lower-class pupils. White children reacted more positively to "church," "house," and "school" than did black children.

Children's views of other peoples are an equally important part of their readiness for social studies and of their ability to deal with the concepts of social studies. Miel and Kiester (234), reporting the attitudes being developed in a typical suburban school system, made clear the striking neglect of opportunities to help children to judge the worth of others, to feel good about themselves, to straighten out the distressing signals they were continually receiving from the society at large, to learn to relate to others, and to manage their own learning more effectively. It is not difficult to see most local communities mirrored in the results of this unusual study. Nor do children's views of foreign peoples outside the pupils' environment paint a brighter picture.

Lambert and Klineberg (207) report an elaborate study of three age samples of 100 each from each of 11 countries. Subjects were individually interviewed to secure their views of their own and other people. The findings suggested several things: The way in which the concept of their group is taught to children has important psychological implications. Early training marks certain groups as outstandingly different. Foreign people seem to be represented as different, strange, and unfriendly. Children in certain groups think of themselves in racial, religious, or national terms; others do not. The study suggests that children's early training has much to do with their particular attitudes toward foreign people and that children are easily influenced by the emotionally-toned opinions of their elders.

In an effort to achieve affective goals, Fisher (103) studied the effect upon fifth-grade pupils of differing treatments designed to affect pupil attitudes toward Indian-Americans. One treatment was based on readings from children's literature; another combined the reading of literature with discussion; a third group served as control. Results favored the treatment groups in the order described above. It is worth noting that the attitudes of black pupils changed more than did those of white pupils.

Johnson (185) carried out a study somewhat related to the matter of understanding other peoples. She tested 179 sixth-grade pupils and 106 university pre-teachers on generalizations regarding South Africa, using a 70-item multiple-choice instrument, *How Much Do You Know About Africa?* Children from middle-class groups achieved slightly but consistently above lower-class subjects. However, 19 stereotyped distractors which were included in the test were accepted by 14 percent of the population studied. The researcher recommended the introduction of Africa's new nations to primary-grade pupils and continued efforts to develop unstereotyped generalizations.

A study by Harris (154) casts an interesting sidelight here. He studied the treatment of religion in elementary school textbooks, finding that textbooks were unduly sectarian in their views. While religious influence in the past was not entirely neglected, the church today was not portrayed as a significant force. In general, religious conflicts and persecutions were not responsibly treated.

Two other studies are related to the problem of values and attitudes but are unrelated to each other. Davis (74) conducted a study to ascertain the ability of 409 fourth-, fifth-, and sixth-grade children to distinguish between statements previously judged to be facts and statements judged to be opinion. Since results showed that only 36 percent of the pupils received a satisfactory score, the researcher recommended that more direct instruction is needed in this area and that teachers also may need direction here.

Perrodin (249) examined factors affecting the development of cooperation in children. The *Behavior Preference Record,* which evaluates pupil preference for certain kinds of social behavior, was administered to 352 children in fourth through eighth grades. Personal data sheets, consisting of 37 items of home, community, and school information, were completed for each subject. Cooperation was defined as the kind of behavior in which the child expresses a preference for helpful, constructive relationships toward others. In the study, boys tended to outscore the girls; home life had a slight effect on children's preferences; participation in certain community organizations had a positive effect; television viewing and extensive reading were characteristics of children who indicated greater preference for cooperative behavior. The researcher pointed out, of course, that further study is needed to determine the relationship of pupils' actual behavior to that expressed as a preference in written situations.

The concern for values and attitudes—the affective domain—will no doubt continue and accelerate as the demands of current society emphasize the need for new social directions. It seems clear that, while researchers do not agree on how the values, attitudes, knowledges, and abilities which have been reviewed in this chapter do develop or when, there is a growing body of research knowledge about pupils upon which to base social studies planning and instruction.

4. Learning and Inquiry in Social Studies

IN SOME elementary classrooms, learning in social studies appears to be little more than the acquisition of information and skills. In other schools, learning in social studies is far more comprehensive, encompassing an awareness of environment and its influences upon people, an understanding of human relationships, an orientation to cultural values, an appreciation of cultural heritage, an empathy for others, and a commitment to democratic ideals and ways of working.

Educational psychologists, of course, define learning more specifically. Blair and others (25) define it as any change of behavior which is a result of experience. Gagné (117) characterizes learning as an alteration in human disposition or capability which can be retained and which is not simply ascribed to the process of growth. In an even more specific sense, Hamachek (146) describes learning as something which is usually followed by a change in behaving, thinking, or feeling. Contemporary investigators support the idea that each individual is the person he has learned to be. All these definitions are pertinent to learning in social studies.

For the teacher of social studies the important question is this one: What are the principal concerns of the teacher regarding learning? Briggs (32), in a study of learning variables in group teaching methods, states that both research and classroom practices encounter confusion with this problem, which has in essence three concerns—the nature of the learner's progress, reasons for his success or failure, and decisions about methods of teaching him. Briggs believes that the first two concerns must precede the third.

In the social studies classroom, learning pervades all activities. Dinkmeyer and Dreikurs (80) remind teachers that children are purposive and striving; they do not merely react; they are active participants in activities that are meaningful to them. Goebel (130) examined the motivational appeal of various learning activities and found that rapid and normal learners were best motivated by reading for discussion and by making vocabulary lists, graphs, and charts. The slow learners rated reading for discussion and

41

map work highest in motivational appeal. However, both groups rated well experiences in dramatizing and mural-making, neither of which appeared to be taught frequently in the schools.

Holt (169) encourages teachers to have more faith in children's learning. He feels that teachers should expose pupils to challenging materials and experiences, give them help and guidance when needed, listen when they talk, and stay out of their way. Bruner (39) similarly supports this point of view with his often-quoted declaration that children can learn any content at any age if it is presented in an intellectually honest form.

Learning as Inquiry

Much of the discussion and research in learning in social studies is related to the development of inquiry skills and an examination of the conditions which promote and encourage discovery and problem solving. Bruner (38) suggests that if students are to learn the techniques of discovery they must be given many opportunities in problem solving. The more practice in problem solving, the more children gain control of the techniques of inquiry.

But what are problem solving, inquiry, and discovery? Sagl (278), in pursuit of a definition of inquiry, attempts to clarify the relationships that exist among the three. She sees problem solving as a process in which learners inquire into possible solutions to their problems and gather data which they organize to facilitate generalizing. In this concept of problem solving, learners are guided to discover relationships among data by engaging in problem-solving experiences that facilitate this discovery. Inquiry is a process in which children study a problem, hypothesize and formulate theories that get at the why and how. The focus is not on established generalizations but on theories that predict what may happen if they are put to the test.

Fenton (100) suggests that a mode of inquiry consists of a number of cognitive skills combined in a logical order. He has identified six essential steps in this process: recognizing a problem from data; formulating hypotheses; recognizing the implications of the hypotheses; gathering data; analyzing, evaluating, and interpreting data; and evaluating the hypotheses in light of the data.

Dwyer (87) proposed a method of ethical inquiry as a model for helping pupils answer the question: What is reasonable for me to believe about what I ought to do as right and what I ought to pursue as good? The steps in the method include identifying the ethical question, isolating the issue at stake, analyzing the meaningfulness of the question, determining the source of the question, clarifying terms, evaluating reasons, examining alternatives, determining practicability, analyzing ethical compatibility, and placing a given belief into one's own value system.

Skills of Inquiry and Problem Solving

Skills and abilities in inquiry and problem solving have been the subject of several research efforts. Harootunian and Tate (151) used 635 seventh- and eighth-grade pupils in a study to determine the relationship of certain variables to problem-solving ability. The variables included problem recognition, word fluency, closure, ideational fluency, judgment, intelligence, and reading. The results showed a high correlation between problem-solving ability and reading and a low correlation with closure and ideational fluency. Frasier (114) used Parsons' construct of four functions which every social system must perform—pattern maintenance, goal attainment, adaptation, and integration—as a basis for a strategy of inquiry to be taught to fourth-, fifth-, and sixth-grade children. Pupils became increasingly able to answer questions clearly related to problem analysis and hypothesis formulation.

Reading skills used in problem solving by fourth-grade pupils were the focus of a study by Robinson (268). The investigator worked individually with 12 pupils of average to superior reading ability. Each subject selected one of two problems created especially for the study and was asked to solve the problem through reading any of the materials surrounding him. Each was to tell aloud what he was doing as he worked in the preparation of a report on the problem he had chosen. The technique used in the study proved to be a fruitful one in revealing the variety of skills used by the pupils and the nature of their strengths and weaknesses. The study suggests that teachers should become aware of the skills their pupils are using, of the skills they need in reading particular content materials and references, and of the need for instruction in skills they do not possess.

Rapparlie (261) involved primary-grade pupils in problem situations, encouraging them to pursue each problem until it was solved or until all avenues of approach were exhausted. Then she led the children to examine the processes they had used, to evaluate their thinking in terms of guidelines or norms, and to plan improvements in strategy. She concluded that under the careful guidance of the teacher such critical thinking skills as observing, comparing, classifying, and analyzing can and should be taught to first- and second-grade pupils.

Acquiring the skills of inquiry has been the center of interest in a number of studies. In several of them a systematic approach has been undertaken. Blank (26) devised auto-instructional procedures to train pupils to ask questions about pertinent facts of a problem before attempting to solve it. Part of the materials dealt with social types of problems. Experimental group one used the auto-instructional unit; those in group two read the same problems in a programmed format but without the inquiry training material; the control group did not see the programs or problems. Data from 54 sixth-grade pupils showed that those in the training program asked more questions and participated more actively in class discussion. The questions asked in this group were proportionately as relevant as those in the other groups.

The main objective of a study by Possien (253) was to compare three methods of developing problem-solving skills, also with sixth-grade pupils. Another purpose was to compare the problem-solving behavior of certain individuals selected from the three groups. The researcher taught each of the groups for 30 minutes a day for three weeks. One group was taught by inductive methods, one group by deductive methods, and the third group by deductive methods with explanations of cause and effect relationships underlying each concept. Possien concluded that pupils using the inductive methods exhibited effective problem-solving behavior more often than pupils taught by the other two approaches.

Suchman (317) trained pupils to formulate questions to determine the parameters of a situation, to determine the relevance of certain conditions, and to experiment verbally to test hypotheses. Suchman concluded that fifth-grade pupils can improve their skills in inquiry and become more productive in their use of questions; as they progress, they make fewer unrelated assumptions; they perform more controlled experiments during the inquiry period; and they become able to transfer their strategies to new problem situations.

Gornick (136) was also interested in transfer of learning and particularly whether or not a conceptual framework would facilitate such transfer in social studies. He selected significant concepts, five each from geography, economics, history, anthropology, and sociology, upon which to base instruction. Concepts were developed with the pupils using various location points around the world;

once identified, each concept was posed as an hypothesis and then tested in different locales. A situation test to assess the extent of transfer yielded results that showed transfer to be greatly enhanced by the conceptual-framework approach.

Carmichael (48) compared a conceptual method based on inquiry and discovery with a textbook approach in developing map skills and geographic understandings. He found that the conceptual method which stressed thinking strategy produced better achievement in map reading and in geographic understandings, though the improvement was statistically significant only for the latter skill. The experimental group was, however, highly motivated and self-directed.

Several researchers have been interested in pupils' ability to make inferences from their learning in social studies, although their results differ. The Joyces (193) taught an experimental group of fourth- and fifth-grade pupils and a control group of fourth-grade pupils through discussion of films of children of other lands. Discussion in the experimental group emphasized what seemed to be important to the families in the films. The control group focused discussion on comparison of the families. Tests indicated that experimental groups developed a more sophisticated appreciation and knowledge of values through their experiences in drawing inferences.

Stitt (314), using ten 50-minute self-instructional lessons designed to teach sixth-grade pupils to recognize warranted inductive and deductive inferences, found clear evidence that the pupils could develop skills of inferential thinking. Weber (338) asked children to interpret a hypothetical map in terms of several factors—population distribution, economic factors, physiological factors, political and military factors, social and cultural factors. He found that in general sixth-grade pupils lacked ability to infer the influence of the environment on man.

The formulation of generalizations based on inquiry has been of concern to researchers because of the apparent difficulty this phase poses for teachers. Greenblatt (139) used eight sixth-grade classes, four experimental and four control, to determine the degree to which pupils could formulate certain generalizations pertaining to the geography of Mexico. The control group followed the usual social studies unit on Mexico, while the experimental group pursued a program designed in terms of major geographical generalizations. All findings indicated that the experimental group scored significantly higher than the control group; pupils in this group brought more information to the solution of problems, revealed fewer misconceptions, and showed deeper understanding of the content. David (71) developed a valid and reliable instrument to measure the ability to generalize and used it in a study to determine the conditions which foster the ability to generalize. The investigator found that teaching-learning situations which encouraged problem solving and active participation by pupils fostered growth in the ability to generalize.

Questioning and Thinking

There is much current writing about the relationship of the teacher's questions to the quality of pupils' thinking. The consensus seems to be that the teacher's skill in questioning may be one of the most important factors in lifting the level of pupils' thinking. Teacher-pupil interaction encompassing the whole atmosphere of classroom interchange has been receiving considerable scrutiny. In social studies, patterns of interaction are particularly crucial as they relate to inquiry and to problem solving.

A study by McNaughton and others (230) was designed to develop teaching modules (definitive sequences of teacher-pupil interaction that result and include high-level pupil thought) to be used in training teachers to improve their questioning patterns. While the researchers felt that the development of high-level thinking by children is partly idiosyncratic on the part of teachers, they found it possible to use the training modules in in-service education in helping teachers build their own questioning strategies. Schreiber's (288) study of teachers' questioning behavior revealed that prior to instruction teachers usually asked factual recall questions, those that called for experience or opinion; after instruction there was an increase in the variety of their questions and in the frequency of questions that encourage inquiry, hypothesizing, problem solving, and generalizing.

Crump (68) obtained similar results through the use of programmed instruction in questioning, confirming the widespread use of recognition and convergent questions before instruction, and finding that instruction improved questioning toward more divergence. Adams (2) also devised a system of classifying teachers' questions and applied it to junior and senior high social studies and English teachers. One interesting result was that social studies teachers used significantly more memory questions and significantly fewer evaluative and clarifying questions than did the teachers of English. One hopeful sign—when Adams compared his results with those of a similar study in 1921, he found that present-day teachers use significantly fewer memory questions.

Three other studies further emphasize the importance of improving teacher skills in questioning. Davis and Hunkins (76) looked at textbooks with a view to discovering the thinking processes they foster, using questions asked in the textbooks as indicators of the quality of thinking sought. The disappointing results of studying three recent fifth-grade textbooks showed that the vast majority of the questions were concerned with knowledge; 78 percent of these knowledge questions dealt with knowledge of specifics. The researchers concluded that textbooks give relatively little emphasis to the development of higher-level thought processes via the questioning technique. Davis and Tinsley (77) also studied the classroom questions asked by social studies student teachers, finding that their questions were very largely of the memory-comprehension variety. Both these studies further stress the importance of increased emphasis upon the asking of questions.

Floyd (105) analyzed the oral activity of 40 "best" teachers, from a random sampling of 40 schools out of a possible 253, teachers with 1,071 pupils in their charge. An hour taped session with each of 30 teachers and a full-day taping with the other 10 provided the data upon which the study was based. Did teachers ask an unusually high number of questions, what kind of questions did they raise, and how good were they? Floyd found that teachers dominated the oral activity, giving pupils little opportunity to do the work themselves. The teachers' questioning techniques encouraged guessing and poor habits of thought, with memorization appearing to be the main goal of instruction. Teachers performed as cross-examiners with little interest in individual pupils and seemed unaware of the value of questions and of appropriate question-asking techniques. These findings simply bear out those previously cited and further point up some crucial needs in teacher education if pupil inquiry is to be encouraged.

Gagnon (118) looked searchingly at questioning in a study designed to help teachers assist pupils in value clarification. After teachers were introduced to value-clarifying techniques, they were encouraged to implement the method in their classroom. The study revealed that, as teachers asked more clarifying questions, they talked less and pupils generally evidenced higher levels of thinking. Moreover, it was clear that pupils also need direct instruction in asking probing, value-type questions.

Other research has approached differently the study of inter-action patterns in the social studies classroom. Herman (158; 159) analyzed the lengths of time pupils engaged in various activi-ties and studied the teacher-pupil interaction during observation of these activities. In each of the achievement-level groups, inter-action described as "teacher lecture with questions" and "teacher questions, pupils answer" comprised about a fourth of the time; directions and commands took about the same amount of time; total pupil talk used about one third of the time; the teacher usually dominated from 40 to 70 percent of the time. In general, teachers of more capable pupils were more indirect in their instruction and more democratic; in this group, pupil-centered activities were more prevalent. Herman (159; 162), also interested in children's use of the language arts in social studies lessons, discovered that 75 per-cent of pupil time was spent in listening, 10 percent in reading, and less than 2 percent in writing. Teacher and pupils were com-municating verbally overall about 40 percent of the time. Herman (159; 161) asked pupils in his study to rank the subjects. Forty-three percent of the pupils, 31.4 percent of them from the above average group, put social studies in last or next to the last place in the list. As teachers in the study became less direct and more open in their planning, pupils liked social studies better.

A noteworthy contribution to the role of teacher questioning has been made by Taba (319), who emphasized strategies which would stimulate certain cognitive processes, encourage certain types of inquiry, and develop basic concepts. Taba saw that, to help pupils progress to higher cognitive levels, teachers must learn the strategy of questioning, not merely asking more divergent questions but sequencing and timing such questions in just the right way to help a particular group of pupils move to higher levels of thought.

A study by Block (27) also was concerned with sequence as a factor in classroom instruction. She recorded 32 social studies and language arts lessons in primary rooms and used them to build a goal-focus-operation model. She identified an "action unit" as a discussion sequence in four steps: the goal or aim, the focus on an idea with which pupils interact verbally, the operation or interaction to approach the goal, and evaluation of the correctness or value of the response. She concluded that definite sequence patterns do exist but that the type of sequence pattern varies for each element of the sequence. It seemed clear that the selection and sequencing of teaching elements are essential components of con-tinuity in learning and are revealed by indexes of pupils' cognitive interaction and progression. This study emphasizes, as did that by Taba, that discussion is something more than a series of questions and responses.

Methods and Techniques That Encourage Inquiry

Methods of encouraging inquiry, problem solving, and critical thinking have been receiving considerable attention in recent research studies. Not only has the role of questioning been explored as noted above, but other techniques and variables have been examined.

Crabtree (60; 61) designed a study to test the influence upon children's thinking of a teacher-structured program versus an unstructured one. Two groups of second-grade children were involved in discussions followed by free-play activity. In the structured program the teacher carefully predetermined the discussion and exposed the children to high environmental structure in the free-play period. In the other program, pupils and teacher cooperatively explored ideas in the discussion; the play period environment contained low realism materials. Data gathered through observation of the play periods showed that divergent thinking was more frequently displayed in the unstructured situation. In a project with a somewhat similar hypothesis, Campbell (45) found that pupils who were encouraged individually and freely to plan and carry out programmed instruction in social studies were more successful in problem solving than were pupils who strictly adhered to the program in its intended sequence.

Goldmark (132) reports a dialogue between teacher and sixth-grade pupils which illustrates those aspects of critical thinking which Goldmark believes go beyond problem solving. The "model" shows the steps in the process and also includes a dialogue in which teacher and pupils inquire about their methods of inquiry. Of special interest in light of foregoing comments are the questions with which the teacher guides the discussion and analysis.

Although the focus of the study was not inquiry, the work of Skov (302), who hypothesized that pupils in a program structured to promote social learnings for democratic behavior would learn more facts and enjoy their learning more, seems to have relevance to the environment of the inquiry-centered classroom. Through a variety of media, Skov collected data from sixth-grade classes characterized by cooperative effort in planning, sharing, purposing, and evaluating, and whose work was based on pupil interests and experiences. Data gathered by means of standardized tests showed that the pupil subjects exceeded the norms for their grade level and exhibited learnings that were more than isolated facts.

A rather unique approach to inquiry in social studies is the concept of "social sciencing" described by Joyce (191; 192) and being demonstrated at the Broad River School in Norwalk, Connecticut. The central purpose of the experiment is to teach children to accumulate data from life situations, to identify patterns of society, and to determine what causes them and how they affect other social groups. The basic materials of this experiment are "data banks," which are index systems used to store anthropological data for a given culture. The original "data banks" for the study were storage systems for information on the old Indian town of La Stella, and on a small New England town named Prestonport. Individually and in small groups, pupils were taught to identify significant questions leading to essential information; to call for the needed data available in a variety of media; and to gather, organize, report, and draw conclusions from the data. Joyce's report describes in detail how one of the boys in the study proceeded through an inquiry experience. The account certainly opens new horizons for developing independent skill in inquiry and problem solving.

Pursuing possible advantages of problem solving, Jones (190) divided 316 fifth-grade children into two matched groups to investigate the relationships which exist between the problems approach and the main-ideas approach to social studies instruction. Tests constructed by the investigator revealed significant differences in favor of the group using the problems approach in the development of abstract concepts; but pupils using the main-ideas approach were more successful in the development of concrete concepts, qualified concepts, qualified abstract concepts, and relevant generalizations.

Four narrative cases related to "lobbying" or "subsidizing" were used by Grannis (137) to study the inductive learning of abstract social concepts by high-achieving sixth-grade pupils. Through formally-structured verbal materials his subjects were asked to react to the cases with certain variables applied. The follow-up test required each subject to recognize new cases as positive or negative applications of the concept and to reverse the cases. In spite of the complexity of the materials and the difficulties experienced in using them, 15 percent of the pupils demonstrated that they had learned the concepts.

Hunkins and Shapiro (172) investigated the usefulness of the case method in encouraging critical thinking. Two classes of similar characteristics were engaged in 16 lessons. In the experimental group, children were forced to take and defend positions based on case studies. Children in the control group were taught by textbook-lecture methods. Only the case study group made gains in critical thinking as identified by the *Behavior Preference Record*.

Hunkins (170; 171) also pursued the problem of critical thinking as influenced by text materials. He was interested in discovering whether the use in text materials of analysis and evaluation questions (as defined by Bloom) would stimulate critical thinking on the part of sixth-grade pupils. The experimental group used such materials; the control group used text materials emphasizing knowledge questions. Surprisingly, however, tests showed no significant difference in critical thinking between the two groups; on the other hand, the group using the higher level questions scored significantly better in social studies achievement. Their success suggests that because they had to be more active in pursuing the divergent questions, they in fact learned the basic information more readily. This study also emphasizes again the potential which questioning holds for social studies instruction.

The encouragement of elaborative thinking engaged the interest of Savage (281), who designed a study to determine whether such thinking was best developed through a group or an individual approach. One hundred twenty-five sixth-grade pupils worked each day on one of ten elaborative thinking exercises, each of which was a situation followed by a question or direction to stimulate thinking. Each child worked on five of the exercises by himself, responding in writing, and on five in groups. The sheer quantity of questions was the measure; and on all exercises the mean number of responses given per individual was smaller than the mean number of responses given by groups on the same exercise. Apparently the group contact influenced significantly the elaborative thinking of individuals.

Other researchers have been looking at the organization of instruction in terms of pupils' learning. Sinks (301) studied the effect of individualization of instruction in social studies at the junior high level. He found that the individualized social studies program of 4½ months' duration resulted not only in favorable achievement test scores but also in social behaviors as well. On the other hand, Jester (184) found no significant results favoring team teaching over departmentalized teaching for eighth-grade students in social studies and language arts. Similarly, Kelly (200), comparing a special coordination of teaching under a master teacher with a conventional organization for teaching social studies at the fifth-grade level, found no significant data favoring the special plan of organization.

Joyce and Weinberg (194) identified four sociological concepts as the basis for a study designed to help third-grade and fifth-grade pupils use strategies of sociology in discovering human relationships. Through small group discussions, the researchers confirmed that pupils could cite examples of each of the concepts— *norms, sanctions, values,* and *roles.* The guiding questions they used proved to be effective in helping pupils identify observable forms of the concepts.

Rusnack (275) reports on three years of experimentation devoted to discovering the limitations in adapting skills and concepts for first-grade pupils. She found that pupils' ability to develop research methods, to make reports and engage in committee work, and to organize information and their ability to understand concepts of historical sequence, cause and effect, geographic space, adaptation to environment, and comparison of simple and complex societies were subject to specific limitations. Inability to read, the need for simplicity, pupils' brevity of attention span, and the need for close direction were identified as the most significant of these limitations.

In spite of the fact that researchers are illuminating aspects of learning and inquiry that may be helpful to teachers, research also continues to produce evidence that teaching in general is not as yet attuned to their findings. For example, Vorreyer's (334) analysis of teachers' classroom behavior uncovered very little variety in basic teacher behavior and very little relationship between pupil achievement and the variety of teacher behavior patterns. At about the same time, Cannon (47) examined teacher perceptions of successful teaching in social studies in the elementary level. From the data it appeared that teachers generally had high regard for readiness, teacher-pupil planning, and specific teaching strategies. They used teacher appraisal to reinforce learning and considered acquisition of knowledge as a factor in evaluation. While these perceptions may not be unrelated to inquiry and problem solving, it is significant that encouragement of critical thinking, development of inquiry skills, and methods of problem solving were not perceived as concerns of the successful teacher of social studies.

5. Educational Media for Social Studies

IN THE classrooms of the past, social studies materials were principally the textbook, maps and globes, and perhaps a set of encyclopedias. Today, however, pupils and teachers are experiencing a whole new concept in media. The availability of instructional aids of many kinds has made it possible for boys and girls to develop data-gathering skills in wide range and to make in-depth studies of increasing significance.

The impetus to inquiry and problem solving made possible by multi-media approaches to learning has been tremendous. Availability of federal funds for such materials has enabled almost every school to enlarge its sources of information far beyond the textbook. Consequently, the selection and use of various media of instruction have been the focus of considerable current research.

Reading Materials

Reading materials used in social studies have, of course, been a continuing target for research, and studies from a variety of points of view have shed some light on their values and usefulness. Readability, understandably, is a prime concern. Arnsdorf (12) analyzed 25 books included in four basal social studies series at both primary and intermediate levels. After application of appropriate reading formulas, he concluded that the readability levels progressed generally in accordance with publishers' intention but that differences between primary and intermediate texts were large. Furthermore, he did not find a consistent progression of difficulty from the beginning to the end of the textbook.

Dusenberry (85) compared older editions (late 1940 or early 1950) and newer editions (late 1950 or 1960) of certain fourth-, fifth-, and sixth-grade social studies textbooks from six publishers and found a discernible improvement in readability to make the text more appropriate for the intended grade level. (The investigator also observed considerable improvement in quantity of illustrative materials.) The readability of selected juvenile encyclopedia materials was studied by Liske (219), who used the *cloze* procedure and compared results with readability formulas. More than 1,000 fourth-, fifth-, and sixth-grade pupils were tested on 15 articles from the 1967 edition of the World Book Encyclopedia. The results indicated that the material was too difficult for the average and below-average pupils. As the publisher had indicated, the difficulty of the longer articles increased from beginning to end; the beginning materials were more easily read by the population tested. Obviously less able pupils may need teacher help and direction in using these materials.

DuVall (86), interested in the ever-increasing quantity of free and inexpensive learning materials, found that 520 teachers of intermediate-grade pupils were able to assign readability levels to four selected pieces of material, although their judgment did not agree with the results secured through a readability formula. Experienced teachers seemed to be more skillful than others in determining whether or not their own pupils could read the materials chosen for the study.

In addition to concern for readability, social studies textbooks have been viewed from many other points of view. While these studies, looked at individually, do not produce overwhelming evidence from which teachers may generalize, nevertheless each of them serves to draw attention to the textbook—its content, its treatment of various values, concepts, and generalizations. The following studies represent the great variety of approaches taken to an analysis of the textbook.

Gillespie (127) compared the content of basal readers and fifth-grade social studies texts, concluding that reading instruction was not adequate for the development of skills needed for social studies content. Differences between the two in treatment, content, and key ideas led her to conclude that skills required for using the two types of textbooks differed significantly.

Chew (55) analyzed the content of selected second-grade social studies textbooks in terms of content relevant to the California generalizations and in terms of cognitive levels of material as related to Bloom's taxonomy of educational objectives. Five of the 19 textbooks were totally unrelated to the generalizations; others demonstrated as much as 74 percent relevancy. Most of the content was at the knowledge level, the lowest level in the Bloom taxonomy. Also interested in content, Kranyik (203) compared the image of Mexico portrayed in elementary social studies textbooks with that possessed by Connecticut and Mexican teachers.

The responses to questionnaires made by the teachers differed greatly from the image presented in 32 textbooks used in the study. The study seemed to indicate that textbooks do not always paint an unbiased picture of life in other cultures.

Other specific concepts have been the subject of investigation in textbooks. For example, Jarolimek and Foster (179) studied in detail three fifth-grade textbooks—one in geography, one in history, and one combining the two—to determine the quantitative concepts pupils were expected to understand. They found six categories of concepts—definite references to quantities of objects, indefinite references to quantities of objects, definite references to space, indefinite references to space, definite references to time, and indefinite references to time. The researchers discovered that many of these concepts were included in the texts; for example, in 10 consecutive pages of one text, there were 162; in another, 272; in another, 416; sometimes there were as many as 30 to 40 on a single page.

In a related study, Lyda and Robinson (223) used Jarolimek and Foster's categories to study quantitative concepts in second-grade social studies textbooks. They found all six categories represented in the three textbooks selected for the study, with indefinite references to quantities of objects most frequent, and definite references to space least used. Above-average pupils understood about three-fourths of the concepts as measured by tests constructed by the researchers; below-average learners understood fewer than one-fourth of the concepts. Both studies emphasized the need for clarifying and teaching quantitative concepts appearing in social studies textbooks at all levels.

Time and space concepts in basal social studies materials were also studied by Arnsdorf (14). Samples from four basal social studies series were selected randomly and subjected to formulas for readability. Results indicated that the number of time terms generally increased with grade level and that space terms were used more frequently than time terms. Arnsdorf (11) also experimented with the rewriting of basal text materials for intermediate grades to replace indefinite expressions with more specific terms. He gave both adjusted and unadjusted selections to 333 pupils in 12 urban classes. Evidence from a test of open-ended questions designed to assess understanding of the content seemed to indicate that reduction of the number of indefinite terms did not affect understanding; and, while understanding increased from grade to grade, cursory answers revealing little understanding were frequent at all levels. The fact that even competent readers had difficulty with the materials reinforced the idea that pupils must be taught specifically how to read social studies materials.

Schomburg (287) studied basic textbooks in fourth-grade and sixth-grade geography adopted in the state of Texas to discover the extent to which they presented and reinforced nine basic geographic concepts identified by the National Council for Geographic Education. He decided that the texts did not systematically develop the concepts and that actually little space was given to their consideration. Most neglected were the basic concepts of cartography. High (166) was concerned with the political science concepts in sixth-grade geography textbooks; she found many such concepts, the major portion falling in the category of world relations. All texts examined included concepts related to freedom, rights, and international cooperation, but there was little emphasis upon the historical development of a system or consideration of factors that determine a system. In most cases democracy was presented as desirable, communism as undesirable.

Johnson (187) analyzed fifth-grade and eighth-grade American history textbooks to discover the treatments given to representative social science ideas. He sought evidence on two questions: How reliably does the content reflect that of the social science disciplines? How adequately does this content ensure that a student might learn what the author intended that he learn? After studying both quantitative and qualitative data, Johnson came to the conclusion that ideas the social scientist held to be important for students were not adequately treated.

There has been a revival of concern recently in the extent to which textbooks exhibit identifiable biases. A number of agencies have been gearing their efforts to bringing about the production of teaching materials that present a true picture of the world and of the contributions of its diverse groups. Harris (154) examined the treatment of religion in 120 elementary school social studies textbooks. His analysis of these books produced evidence of strong sectarian tendencies, with the balance in favor of Christianity so pronounced as to be unfair; the textbooks gave modern-day religions little importance in promoting the welfare of society; and they generally lacked objectivity in dealing with persecutions, often neglecting to present both sides of a conflict.

Perrone (250) studied the image of Latin America which children acquire from their textbooks. He found that the pupils clearly exhibited the unflattering views which their textbooks held.

He concluded that improving the quality of text materials may in the long run be of the greatest importance in correcting misconceptions and decreasing prejudice. Lemmond (216) found that textbook publishers needed to consider also the presentation of a more balanced type of value-oriented materials. He analyzed the contents of four fifth-grade textbooks published within the past 40 years and five currently adopted texts. He concluded that the older books placed emphasis on such things as wealth and power, while the newer books gave greater attention to respect for peoples' ways of living and their values. All of the newer books placed less emphasis upon the correctness of moral values particular to a certain culture and were slanted toward understandings of all values considered important to each culture. Lemmond warned that unless publishing trends are altered, textbooks are likely to continue neglecting values of affection, rectitude, enlightenment, and well-being.

Golden (131) studied the treatment of Negroes, American Indians, Orientals, European immigrants, and Jews in the 13 primary social studies texts most widely used in the United States in 1964. The findings were significant. There were no minority groups in six of the texts and no minority group persons in any of the first-grade families in any of the texts. (Sadly enough, in infrequently used books minority group family life was more frequently presented.) In the particular case of black Americans, no adult was named or given a speaking role or pictured in clothes other than occupational uniform.

Banks (18) developed a technique for determining dominant themes used to discuss black Americans and race relations in American history books used in the intermediate grades. The researcher concluded that authors of textbooks usually do not take a moral stand on issues nor do they stress the values of good race relations. He noted improvement in frequency with which textbooks depict achievements of black Americans, but he did not find attention being given to the plight of deprived Americans.

Zimmerman's (351) analysis of famous persons included in six most-used series of intermediate-grade social studies textbooks revealed that 95 percent of the persons identified were white and very few of them were African or Asian or representative of the 20th century. Such studies as these only point up the need for producing social studies materials that are truly responsive to current concern for intergroup and intercultural understanding.

The intensive study that textbooks have been receiving suggests that selecting suitable textual materials poses a serious problem. Two studies throw light on the selection task. Concern for readability of social studies materials led Allbaugh (5) to investigate the relationship between a reading formula and reading comprehension in selected materials. She concluded that use of a formula is valid but also noted that the fact burden of social studies materials requires special consideration. Of interest to selection committees is the report by Willett (347), who describes the development and testing of a method based on a five-point procedure. Available materials were screened on the basis of criteria selected by the users, tested competitively in the classroom, submitted to teacher reaction, and judged by a special committee. Final decision was then made by an adoption committee in the central school office.

The use of programmed materials is appearing in all areas of the curriculum and has made some contributions to social studies instruction, although reactions to them have ranged from enthusiasm to out-and-out opposition. Certainly current interest in the inquiry process colors the attitudes of those who are making decisions about the use of programmed materials. Newmann (245) suggests evaluating programs in terms of Bloom's taxonomy of educational objectives and Ennis' categories of critical thinking. Using excerpts from three programs, Newmann illustrates how analysis of frames of a given program can reveal the cognitive operations demanded. Ryan (277) used linear programs on the geographical features of Japan, constructed for fourth-grade pupils, to test four methods of using programmed materials. One group read through the materials with a teacher aide, another with the classroom teacher. A third group worked through the program in the conventional manner, independently. The control group had no instruction of any kind. Members of the two groups who were aided by teachers achieved at a high level on a post-test; the fact that both good and poor readers achieved considerably better than those in the control group seemed to indicate that reading the program with a teacher had some positive effects over and beyond needed assistance in reading.

Thomas (326), comparing programmed instruction and conventional instruction at the fifth-grade level on content drawn from the Anthropology Curriculum Project at the University of Georgia, found that the chief advantage of the programmed instruction was in the shorter time required to teach the selected information about methods of archaeology. Ryan (276) used programmed materials with four other groups with different variables involved. In this aspect of the study, three groups used the programs supplemented by textbook reading or map work. The fourth group used the program by itself. The groups using the supplemented programs scored higher on the achievement test than the group using the program alone. Results seemed to suggest the wisdom of integrating programmed instruction with other teaching techniques. Tali (325) used *How a Bill Becomes a Law,* a linear program, with 227 junior high pupils. He found that pupils did learn from the experience, with gains from pretest to post-test consistently greater for pupils of high intelligence. The program seemed best suited to pupils of average or above-average performance who were able to work independently.

Farber (98) developed a 161-frame program comparing certain aspects of legislative and executive branches of government in the United States, France, and England for use with 132 eighth-grade pupils. He wished to investigate the use of this program in a group situation to discover the possible values to be secured from group reinforcement or individual reinforcement of correct responses. In one treatment, the learning team was promised a reward for good performances; in another team treatment, rewards were offered individuals; in the third team treatment, there were no rewards. A control group did not use the program. The data from pre- and post-tests showed that all treatment groups performed better than the control group and that team or individual reinforcement had no influence.

Supplementary and collateral materials are, of course, of continuing interest to social studies teachers, as is the research related to them. Anderson (7) contributed considerable knowledge to this area by deriving a list of 213 common topics from more than 100 elementary social studies textbooks and selecting for this list 2,493 titles of supplementary materials which met his standards of selection. Heil (155), convinced of the values of children's literature in the social studies, developed nine categories for clarifying the values of such resources and applied them to wonder tales appropriate for the primary grades. Having made a case for the use of these materials, she developed and included in the report of her study suggestions for their use by teachers.

Thompson (327) used fifth-grade pupils to study the effect of using supplementary materials in economics in both structured and unstructured ways. One group used specific questions keyed to concepts; another group stressed the concepts but did not use the questions; the third group was guided to use the materials whenever useful in the regular economics curriculum; there was a control group which was not subjected to any of the treatments. Results favored the group using the materials in the least-structured way.

Several government-sponsored projects are adding to the reservoir of carefully selected and tested teaching materials in significant areas of social studies content. Gibson (123) has directed a project devoted to the development of instructional materials pertaining to racial and cultural diversity in American society. Gill and Conroy (126) developed guidelines and resource materials for use in the study of Latin America throughout the elementary and secondary school. Involvement of social scientists and those with intimate knowledge of Latin America has added to the value and authenticity of the materials.

Similarly, first-grade materials on family life in Japan were the outcome of a project directed by Arnoff (9). An elaborate survey of hundreds of free materials on conservation led Johnson and Dambach (186) to the conclusion that, unfortunately, conservation materials currently available are highly technical, produced largely for other than school pupils, and fail to touch current conservation problems forcefully. He discovered that teachers were prone to select materials more often on the basis of appearance than content and that the quality of the materials was differently assessed by conservation experts and by teachers.

Visual and Audio Materials

Earlier research has rather effectively demonstrated the learning possibilities in visual and audio teaching materials, but there continues to be research exploring specific facets of the use of these instructional aids in social studies. Cammarota (44) found that certain films and filmstrips designed for use in the intermediate grades were more appropriate for use in the primary grades, this evidence seeming to illustrate that film makers need to be more knowledgeable about the interest level and intellectual capacity of elementary school pupils.

Ingli (173) confirmed earlier research which showed that pupils profit from film techniques. After subjecting fourth- and fifth-grade pupils to both film and nonfilm teaching techniques, the researcher found that the film technique increased factual learning and vocabulary for both groups. Only the fifth-grade pupils, however, showed an advantage in thinking ability and retention of learning at the end of the year. Arnsdorf (13) involved 234 fifth-grade pupils in a six-week instructional program in which he used projected maps to teach understandings of the distribution and interrelationship of physical, biotic, and cultural features. The researcher found the map overlays useful in developing map skills and geographic understandings; gains made by the children were even greater than expected. Based on a study of middle-grade children, Fortess (108) devised a guide to the use of paintings as resources in social studies. She found that paintings which depicted real-life situations were more effective than those which were more abstract in content.

The effectiveness of teaching a social studies unit by short-wave radio was tested by Uslan (332). One group of fifth-grade pupils was taught by radio and the other in the usual social studies program suggested by the state. The experimental group met three times weekly, 40 minutes each meeting, for 16 weeks, while the control group followed their usual routine. Results from specially-designed tests favored the group taught by radio. The reader may raise a question concerning the nature of the instruction, since unaccounted-for variables other than the medium may be important here.

Karns (199) examined the attitudes of teacher and pupils toward television as a source of data compared to the textbook. Forty-four sixth-grade classes listened to videotaped presentations of life in Africa told by Africans and examined other authority sources in comparison. At the conclusion of the "telesson" series the attitudes of teachers and pupils were assessed. Both selected the "telessons" as more authoritative than text materials.

Other Educational Media

The interest in simulation, gaming, and role playing is a fairly new one in social studies, with little research as yet to indicate the values of these experiences. One such effort, however, is the study by Wing (348), who engaged 25 sixth-grade pupils in two computer-based economics games while a control group received conventional instruction. Not only were the games initially as effective as the conventional instruction, but they also led to longer retention of the principles studied.

At the secondary level Boocock (29) and Cherryholmes (54) report research evidence that simulation games were more effective than ordinary classroom methods in arousing pupil interest and involving them in learning. Baker (17) compared textbook and simulation approaches in teaching eighth-grade American history. The simulation presented the problems of the United States during the years between 1840 and 1960 in the structure of international politics. The control group used a textbook-study method. All groups were taught by the researcher. The post-test of learning, the retention test, and the attitude analysis in all cases favored the experimental classes.

Teachers interested in simulation games will find useful a bibliography on simulation prepared by the Foreign Policy Association (106). *Seal Hunting* and *Caribou Hunting* are two for fifth grade from Education Development Center, Cambridge, Massachusetts; *Sierra Leone* and *The Sumerian Game* are two for elementary pupils from the Board of Cooperative Education Services, Yorktown Heights, New York; *Githaka* and *The Market Place* are two others for elementary children, available from CBS Learning Center, Princeton Junction, New Jersey; and another, *Market*, can be secured from the Industrial Relations Center, University of Chicago, Chicago, Illinois. Of particular interest to teachers who are involving their pupils in urban studies is *The City Game* reported by Unruh (331) and recently used in University City, Missouri. In this simulation, pupils are asked to determine action to be taken to remake a city harassed by typical urban problems.

Educational games of the more familiar type were previously studied by Mountain (241), who asked 16 teachers to test 100 games—commercial, noncommercial, or originals and adaptations by the researcher. The study confirmed Mountain's belief that well-selected educational games can be effective teaching aids, can provide purposeful learning experiences throughout elementary and secondary school, and can stimulate and hold pupil interest. Mountain's study includes detailed descriptions of the games and suggestions for their use.

Closely related to and frequently an integral part of simulation are role playing and informal dramatization, each of which has been a part of social studies instruction for a somewhat longer time. Early in the decade Cristiani (65) studied the interest and degree of difficulty sixth-grade children associated with 180 situations based on social studies content. From these Cristiani selected 20 situations to be used in such a way that all pupils in eight classes took part in dramatizing at least one. While there was little difference in achievement scores with or without dramatizations, there was a significant gain on the social acceptance scale and improvement in interest in and attitude toward social studies. Perhaps the biggest impetus to role playing has been given by the Shaftels (297). Their fascinating volume developed from much experimentation not only describes in detail the process of role playing but includes a complete series of open-ended episodes which foster the exploration of social values.

Other studies have further called attention to the benefits of direct involvement of pupils in their learning experiences. Although the theory of social studies instruction has long accepted the idea of direct experiences, the fact that the textbook still remains in such a dominant role in the classroom indicates that continuing research will not be out of place. Schiller (283) found that seventh-grade pupils who made systematic and functional use of work-study skills in social studies achieved greater mastery than pupils who made only incidental use of the skills. The importance of helping pupils to see purpose for learning skills is perhaps most significant here.

Community resources and pupils' use of them were of interest to two other researchers. Forster (107) designed a study to evaluate the field trip as an aid to concept formation. Two fourth-grade social studies classes studied selected topics in their textbook; the experimental group then followed this study with an appropriate field trip; the control group engaged in other worthwhile activity; groups were rotated through four topics. Groups evidenced a greater degree of learning as a result of three of the four field trips, but on no test item were results significantly in favor of field trip groups. There was, however, considerable evidence of interest on the part of the experimental groups. Two groups of sixth-grade pupils directed by Hardy (150) followed a similar plan of instruction in an archaeological study, except that one group concluded its learning experiences with participation in an archaeological dig, while the other was taught in the usual way what the pupils on the dig learned through discovery. The results on a teacher-made test provided evidence of the value of the direct involvement in the discovery process as developed on the dig.

Other resources have also been subjects of research. White (346) undertook a study to determine conservation understandings desirable for grades four through eight and to identify community resources available to develop such understandings. For certain of the main ideas he found field trips; for others, there were useful resource personnel and supplementary materials. Dufty (84) studied on a theoretical basis the values of using folksongs of the United States and Australia in the social studies classroom. Judging from this pre-experimental study, the investigator concluded that folksongs can provide insights into the life of the ordinary man and help to fill in his written history, and that they can help pupils develop appreciation for other people. He recommends a variety of research and cooperative efforts to test this theory.

Comparative Studies of Methods and Techniques

Several studies of a comparative nature have implications for the selection and use of teaching materials. For example, Lux (222), in a study of superior and non-superior teachers, found that highly-rated teachers favored topical over chronological approaches to social studies and more frequently used the problem method and a variety of individual and group activities. Although Lux stressed that perhaps the teacher is more important than the method, nevertheless, superior teachers in his study were teaching social studies in ways that clearly drew upon varied educational media.

Jefferds (183) used economics materials in three ways with primary children. One group used as directed packaged materials from the Senesh work in economics, Our Working World; one group used the same materials as supplementary resources; a third group received regular instruction in the same content by techniques planned by teachers in an in-service program. Follow-up tests revealed that there were no significant differences among the three groups.

The problems of teaching current events to elementary school pupils intrigued Slan (303) into a study comparing the use of an adult daily newspaper with the use of a commercial classroom newspaper in fourth, fifth, and sixth grades. Two classes at each level were matched; once a week for 10 weeks one class in each pair used the adult paper, and the other used the classroom paper. Tests of knowledge of national and world affairs and of ability to read the adult newspaper favored fifth- and sixth-grade pupils who used the adult newspaper. The adult newspaper seemed of limited value in the fourth grade.

Somewhat earlier, Schminke (285) had used 18 sixth-grade classes to test the effectiveness of two methods of using a news magazine in teaching current events. One method was a systematic use of the news magazine as the single resource; the other method used the magazine with optional additional resources. A specific purpose was the focus of presentation and discussion each week. Statistics did not produce a significant difference between the two methods.

In a related effort Smith (306) also used sixth-grade children to develop a simple instructional plan in which pupils devoted practically all of their current events time allotment to direct discussion. Pupils used a commercially-prepared classroom newspaper selected because it was fully devoted to current affairs. Pupils prepared out of class, giving their first attention to two self-selected articles and then pursuing additional information as they chose. Three approaches were used for variety: teacher-led discussion, student panel presentation, and discussion based on individual student outlines placed on the chalkboard. Observers, using a discussion response scale and recording verbatim accounts of discussion, provided data from which the following conclusions were drawn. Sixth-grade pupils' responses in discussions varied with the nature of the event—its remoteness leading to a dependence on facts, its nearness encouraging reflection and free exchange of ideas. Pupils were found to be thoughtful and reflective and to exercise care in framing opinions. They varied widely in their interest in various events, but their discussions were maintained at a higher level of interest and thought when sustained by skillful teacher comment and question.

Watts (337) compared the use of five presentation models of certain geographical terms. Randomly selected pupils from five sixth-grade classes were assigned to five instructional groups. One of the following aids was used in each group: verbal definition, photographs, filmstrips, diagrammatic transparencies, or three-dimensional models. Statistically significant gains were made by groups using diagrammatic transparencies and three-dimensional models when compared with groups using photographs and verbal definitions and also by the filmstrip group when compared with the verbal definition group. Degrees of concreteness of presentation seemed to relate positively to gains made. Buckley (41) evaluated two techniques for teaching social studies generalizations, one based on the Venn diagrams familiar to mathematics students, and the other utilizing list tabulations. He found that the two procedures did not differ significantly in the results they produced.

Weinswig (339) conducted a study to determine whether or not fourth-grade pupils could learn introductory map skills best by working with especially prepared materials independently, in pairs, or in trios. All groups used the lesson materials successfully, with greatest gains made by the groups of three and the least by those working alone. With a somewhat related interest Rich (267) also investigated pupil achievement as related to study groups of varying sizes. Following a mass presentation of social studies content, fourth-, fifth-, and sixth-grade children were organized for follow-up study in teams of three or five or as individuals. All pupils rotated through the variations in group size; and all had access to films, filmstrips, and recordings. For the subjects as a total group, the size of the study team made no significant difference in achievement, although the fourth-grade results slightly favored the three grouping, and both fifth and sixth favored working alone. Films were more popular than filmstrips or recordings; filmstrips were more favored than recordings. Despite, however, the somewhat inconclusive results of the study, the researcher commented favorably on pupils' high level of interest in the follow-up teamwork.

The impact of various media upon social studies instruction has spurred school systems to expand their resources and to offer improved assistance to teachers. Ingraham (174) illustrates the process by which New York City schools organized faculty and publishers to produce media kits for instruction in kindergarten, first, fifth, and sixth grades in 650 schools. With government funds, Brown (36) has developed media guides to encourage the enrichment of social studies through the use of the arts and humanities. The guides develop teaching strategies for the utilization of a wide variety of educational media. The possibilities are so intriguing that few teachers could resist them.

6. Evaluation in Social Studies

EVALUATION is an essential part of any academic program. This idea confronts the reader time and again as he studies plans for curriculum development or innovations in teaching. While it has been and continues to be a matter of concern for many who are interested in innovation and improvement in instruction in social studies, evaluation has not been a widely-researched topic.

A decade ago, however, Allen (6) conducted a national survey of the evaluation behaviors of classroom teachers. His findings were not a cause for optimism. More than 600 members of the National Council for the Social Studies responded to queries about what should be evaluated and what kinds of techniques would be appropriate. The researcher concluded that teachers generally do not evaluate in terms of their objectives, do not take advantage of a full range of possible techniques, do not understand the purposes of evaluation, do not have an adequate knowledge of statistics, and do place great emphasis upon evaluation procedures that yield a grade. There is little evidence that evaluation has improved in quality since this research was undertaken. After a 1965-66 study of educational practices of elementary teachers in Maryland, Duffey (83) concluded that evaluation has never been done really well in the elementary school, that grading dominates evaluation, and that unclear objectives defeat the process of evaluation.

Fraser (111: 576), who directs a yearly review of curriculum materials for the National Council for the Social Studies, after her most recent survey of curriculum guides produced by state and local school systems, comments:

Suggestions for means of evaluating pupils' progress toward stated social studies goals continue to be a neglected area in many of the guides. Indeed, as in previous years, panel members found the lack of clearly defined goals and of related evaluative measures to be the major weaknesses in the current group of guides.

Some disturbing evidence relevant to the relationship of evaluation practices in classroom to goals was uncovered by Tufte (329), who explored the use of higher-level questions by teachers in evaluating attitudes in elementary social studies. He found that all groups investigated favored goals emphasizing attitudes and appreciations and favored the open-ended question as an evaluation device. But when the teachers were asked to formulate their own evaluation questions, they did not adhere to these original positions. Unfortunately, instruction in a methods course did not change the situation.

Some writers on the subject of evaluation explain the lack of effective valuation tools in social studies by pointing out that many of the aspects of growth educators would like to evaluate are rather elusive. How does one know he has effectively measured change or growth in attitudes? How does one determine what the long-range effects of changes will be?

Gall (120) pursues the matter in a discussion of some changes taking place in the area of social studies, emphasizing that the entire instructional program should receive its direction from desired behavioral objectives—whether or not pupils think better, solve problems more efficiently, engage in more profitable and more creative activities, get along with people more effectively. To determine these gains, innovative evaluation schemes will be needed.

Paper and pencil evaluation devices have long been the standard form for assessment; and for many of the inquiries teachers make about pupils such devices may be quite adequate, particularly if the emphasis is upon information and knowledge. But, for the most part, such tests do not result in the kinds of data that authorities in the field are seeking. The difficult task of inventing more effective data-producing techniques faces all those interested in improving social studies instruction.

Promising Techniques in Evaluation

Some of the most interesting efforts in evaluation are related to research studies which themselves are not centered directly upon problems of evaluation. These studies are planned as attempts to find out something about pupils—their behaviors, their reactions, their attitudes, their skills and abilities; but in the process of finding out, evaluation devices are imperatives. Some interesting ones are growing out of these research needs.

For example, current interest in interaction analysis is showing teachers and researchers that techniques of observation may be adjusted and refined for a variety of evaluation situations. A study by Herman (158) uses the interaction analysis technique itself to discover the relationship between teachers' verbal behavior and children's interests in the social studies. While there may be, the researcher says, other reasons for children's reactions to social studies, the positive relationship of the teacher's verbal patterns could have been determined in no way other than by observation.

Crabtree (61), in comparing children taught in a highly-structured program with others who were taught in a problem-solving-inquiry situation, "tested" the subjects by observing them in a free-play environment equipped with objects related to the content of the study. Her evaluation scheme included a teacher observation schedule, describing the teacher's behavior with respect to convergence and divergence; a children's observation scale of behavior, characteristics of divergent thinking and of conceptual thinking (convergent); and a children's involvement scale. These instruments offer useful suggestions for similar observation guides.

The rating scale was used by Raths (262) in a study which attempted, through a process of clarifying values, to improve pupil participation in classroom situations. In brief, the clarifying procedures were those which helped pupils through writing, through individual confrontation, and through class discussion to freely state values, reflect upon them, affirm or reject them. The evaluation procedure, which is of interest at this point, was based upon five dimensions of involvement—the raising of questions and alternatives, initiation and self-direction of classroom activity, perseverance, active participation, and attitudes toward learning. The 100 students were rated before and after the study by special teachers of art, music, physical education, and library, none of whom had been previously apprised of the study. These teachers used a rating scale, which contained a seven-inch line for each dimension, marked at each end with an extreme statement—for example, *very often* to *almost never*. The teacher placed an X along the line, and the distance in inches from the low point became the measure of involvement on that dimension, and the pupil's score the sum of the distances as rated by each of the special teachers.

Gall (119) describes a rating instrument used to evaluate the affective aspect of learning. The instrument consists of 10 statements that could be descriptive of a pupil's reaction when confronted with the task of making a decision, a judgment, or a policy. The statements range from "[The child] is unable to identify alternatives for making choices" to "[The child] has intuitive sense of judgment. Offers unique and original patterns of action. Acts not only wisely, but timely." The teacher records the situation in which the judgment was made and the nature of the child's behavior.

A rating scale was used by pupils in a study by Easton and Dennis (88) in an effort to determine children's image of government. The researchers asked pupils to "think of government as it really is" and to circle the number of their choice on a rating scale. For example, one of the scales contained these items from left to right: "[government] almost never makes mistakes; rarely makes mistakes; often makes mistakes; usually makes mistakes; almost always makes mistakes."

A multiple-choice interest inventory was used by Herman (160) to determine pupil preference for arithmetic, English, science, social studies, and spelling. The inventory consisted of 40 groupings of three typical classroom activities (for example—Give a talk on the U.S. government), and pupils were asked to identify which of the three activities they liked best and which least.

The individual interview, a technique used by Raths as mentioned earlier, was used also by Spodek (311). In order to test his idea that kindergarten children could begin to attain important social studies concepts that would serve as a basis for further development, he involved them in a study of the harbor of New York. To collect evidence of pupils' ability to attain the selected social studies concepts, Spodek devised an interview-test in which pictures and models were used as stimuli.

The question, "Who are you?" was used by Lambert and Klineberg (207) as the focal point for pupil interviews designed to reveal children's views of foreign peoples. Following the first question, the matter was pursued with "What else are you? What else are you? Anything else?" (as needed). Next, pupils were asked to talk about people of eight foreign countries, telling whether or not they liked them and how they had learned about these people. Later in the interview pupils identified the country they would like best if they could not be from their own country and which country they liked least. Information was coded in terms of specific content and evaluative features.

Weber (338) used an interview technique in which pupils studied the hypothetical map of a country and discussed environmental influences on population distribution, economic factors, physiological and health factors, political and military factors, and social and cultural factors.

Rogers and Long (271) used a situation to probe social

sensitivity, a technique which seems to have considerable potential for classroom adaptation. Pupils were told that they were to decide to whom they would contribute $10 in a given "help-needed" circumstance. The locales for the distress events were local, national, or international. Pupils chose the recipients and then reported in discussion or writing why they gave their money as they did. This type of assessment has particular value because the high level of pupil involvement is likely to result in more valid estimates of the characteristic being studied.

Gornick (136) used a situation test also in assessing pupils' ability to transfer learning. After developing basic concepts from the social sciences using various locales around the world, the researcher asked pupils to respond to a situation in a new and unstudied locale in terms of the learning they had already acquired.

Some researchers in social studies have found it necessary to devise specific tests for their studies. Some of these may suggest adaptations by persons who have similar needs. For example, Larkins (208) set out to determine pupils' success in an economics program for the first grade. Because formal tests had not yet been devised for the program, Larkins developed a primary economics test for his particular purpose. Gill (124) devised an interesting test of eighth-grade pupils' knowledge of indefinite quantitative concepts. He selected from textbooks 25 phrases which pupils were asked to interpret concretely. Such terms as *large* sums of money, *tallest* skyscraper, *tens of thousands* of men, a *few* national parks prompted pupils to respond in ways that indicated that their information was strikingly nebulous and erroneous.

As a measure of children's awareness of selected concepts in physical geography, Sheridan (298) asked first-grade children to look at sets of pictures, each set designed to test the pupils' ability to recognize the concept. From a set of eight pictures, pupils were to identify four that represented the concept and four that did not. This test is another example of one which the classroom teacher might use or adapt to gather knowledge about his pupils.

To test second-grade children's understandings of time relationship, McAulay (229) asked pupils to respond to questions designed to reveal their maturity: Who do you think has lived longer, your mother or your grandmother? Which will be here first, Christmas or Easter? Who lived first, Washington or Lincoln? A series of questions like these also has intriguing possibilities for the classroom teacher.

To test time relationships, Chase (52) asked fifth- and sixth-grade pupils to respond to a test of 24 questions requiring the respondent to place in chronological order five items given in each question. The questions, originally developed by Mary G. Callahan, touched four categories: past items or events related to each other or to a given present event or artifact; past events or artifacts unrelated to each other but related to a given present event or artifact; related past events or artifacts without a present one being given; and unrelated past events or artifacts without a present one being given.

Kirsch (201) attempted to assess levels of cognitive learning by fifth-grade classes by devising three methods of evaluation—two multiple-choice tests, one of knowledge and comprehension and one of ability to make application of knowledge and understanding to other situations; individual tape-recorded interviews in which pupils' understanding of the area could be probed more deeply; and observation of the teachers to determine the relationship between teacher behavior and pupil performance. The use of these varying methods points up the desirability and necessity of approaching from different angles the assessment of some of the components of critical thinking.

David (71), who investigated the conditions that foster growth in children's ability to generalize in elementary school social studies, constructed a measuring instrument consisting of 10 open-ended lead questions to solicit the child's essay responses and multiple-choice selections, a set of data to accompany each question, and four alternative choices from which to make a selection. For example, the first question was, "Land is terribly important to people. If this is true, what else can be said about it?" Teacher and pupils then looked at all the related data (a map of the world showing latitudes of various countries, statements about the productiveness of land in Egypt, pictures of two corn crops of differing production and information about the soil treatment of each, two pictures of irrigated land, a picture of rugged mountains and a comment about the difficulty of farming, and the like). Then the original question with four alternatives was presented, with one of the responses representing the acceptable generalization. David evaluated this technique as a successful one in judging pupils' ability to formulate generalizations from data.

There have been few research efforts, apart from those of commercial test builders, to develop special tests. One such test, however, designed as a concept prerequisite and development appraisal, evaluates pupils' ability to attend to a talk, to logically remember, to detect similarities and differences, and the ability to use these skills in conceptualizing. Brown (34), who successfully developed the test for young pupils, suggests that it could be standardized for use with older pupils as well.

Henson (156) developed a 60-item test of social studies achievement for the first four elementary grades. The test, designed to measure concepts, skills, knowledges, and understandings, was successfully validated and proved to be reliable. The procedures used and the test itself may be of interest to those who have a similar evaluation task to perform.

Hills (168), in order to study children's learnings about social studies generalizations, developed a *Dimensions of Learning Test,* designed as a test of terminology and application. Hills concluded that children's acquisition of generalizations can be measured in part by tests, but that terminology and application items measure different aspects of learning.

Taba and others (323: 77), as a facet of their study of children's thinking, developed a *Social Science Inference Test,* designed to assess "the ability to discriminate between the various items given in the test problem, to draw inferences or 'to go beyond that which is given,' to recognize the limits of the data, and to refrain from overgeneralizing or from being over-cautious"; and to determine "the tendency to make errors which represent contradictions to what the data tell or suggest." The test consists of items each describing a situation in which behaviors or events are interrelated and each with a number of choices which are inferences varying in their degree of plausibility or probability of occurrence. If the child understands the generalization on which the item is built, he will be able to make appropriate inferences. The test yields scores on discrimination, inference, caution, and overgeneralizing.

Goolsby (135), interested in finding out whether or not social studies tests designed to test a specific outcome are justifiable, developed a study to determine the interrelationships among seven measures of competency in elementary social studies. He gave 555 Iowa eighth-grade pupils four tests drawn from a battery of standardized tests: reading social studies materials, map reading, reading of graphs and tables, knowledge of and use of references; and three tests organized especially for this study: judgment and critical thinking, knowledge of facts, and understanding of terms. The quite high intercorrelations among the tests and the very little unique variance among them led Goolsby to conclude that there is little justification for differentiating among tests for these outcomes, unless using separate tests is for the convenience of teachers in preparing pupils for the tests and for reviewing them afterwards.

Expert Approaches to Evaluation

Although there seems to be a dearth of research specifically related to the development of improved evaluation techniques, writers in the field have not been silent. Examination of recent articles related to evaluation in the social studies, discussion in recently published texts, as well as entire volumes which relate to evaluation, highlight items useful as guidelines and some techniques that may prove highly beneficial in the development of evaluation devices. Some of these are presented here in lieu of evidence supported by research.

Gardner and Warmke (121), who are primarily interested in economics, have made suggestions which seem applicable to evaluation in other areas of social studies. They list certain subjective procedures for evaluating any program under scrutiny—getting the judgment of experts, collecting feedback from teachers and pupils, and using trained observers. For less subjective evaluation, they suggest a combination of testing devices: standardized tests to measure cognitive areas; pretests and post-tests with item analysis; and word associations—concept words to which students are asked to respond by writing words of which they are reminded. Cornish (58) is convinced that teachers carry on many activities simply because they think they are worthwhile. He emphasizes the importance of evaluating the acquisition of concepts and generalizations (a process that is much more difficult than evaluation of facts and relationships) through behavior rating scales, teacher-made tests, sociodramas, and conferences.

Ragan and McAulay (260) identify the purposes of evaluation—to provide a basis for individual guidance, to determine what understandings the pupil has gained, to improve methods and materials, to inform the pupil of his progress, to help him judge his own progress, and to improve group work. Clements and others (56) point out that evaluation serves another rather striking and important purpose, at least from the pupil's point of view: it tells the pupil what the teacher thinks is important. In other words, when the teacher's evaluation technique emphasizes aspects of inquiry, pupils know that inquiry is considered important; when facts or textbook memorization are tested, the pupil knows what is important and what he must do to fare well in the evaluation. Servey

(296) strongly supports the importance of encouraging growth in inquiry with evaluation techniques which place the emphasis upon it. He outlines several clues for teachers which he puts into two categories: inquiry into facts and ideas and inquiry into attitudes and patterns of behavior. For these purposes, he recommends use of mental notes, observation sheets, anecdotal records, and informal tests. In evaluating children's performance relative to attitudes and patterns of action, he suggests creative projection, dramatization, open discussion of a problem or situation, and sometimes projects that grow out of inquiry.

A number of other writers in the field give special attention to the evaluation of critical thinking or its various facets. The Thirty-Fifth Yearbook of the National Council for the Social Studies has several contributors who share this concern. Chausow (23: 77-79), after emphasizing the importance of critical thinking, says teachers should test students' ability to identify basic assumptions, identify central issues, evaluate evidence, and determine whether conclusions are warranted. While he illustrates variations in the type of responses that might be elicited, his suggested technique is the use of objective tests.

Mayhew (23: 115-36) says that teachers must make quite clear what behavior they are evaluating and must understand clearly the object or attributes of the object about which opinions are being solicited. He cautions them to choose carefully the words used; to refrain from preparing more questions than can be used and interpreted; to revise questions after letting them stand for a few days; and, after administering a set of questions, to tabulate the results, discuss them with the class, and leave the matter. He would supplement tests with a variety of other devices, most of which have been mentioned earlier in this review. Dunfee (23: 154-73) lists specific ways to evaluate understandings, attitudes, and behaviors, but she emphasizes that the final evaluation will be the way in which the individual applies to everyday living what he has learned.

Standardized tests have long been recognized as instruments for measuring cognitive aspects of children's growth in social studies, but few instruments really evaluate higher levels of cognitive behavior and most do not touch the affective aspect of growth. The *Sequential Tests of Educational Progress* (295) in social studies are examples of tests built on the premise that what a pupil can do with his knowledge is as important as what he knows. The tests involve pupils in verbal situations to which they must respond in terms of basic understandings in social studies and which require them to utilize skills in interpreting data; in seeing relationships among facts, concepts, and ideas learned; in recognizing bias and attitudes; in distinguishing among opinion, fact, and propaganda; in determining the adequacy of data; in applying appropriate outside information and criteria; and in drawing valid conclusions.

Curriculum Evaluation

There is little evidence at present of research directed toward the evaluation of curriculum programs in social studies. However, the proposal for national assessment of social studies must be considered important to curriculum planners. The purpose of the assessment is to find out what pupils of four different ages (nine, twelve, seventeen, and adult), from different geographical regions, and from varying socioeconomic levels know about social studies. The evaluation is based upon five objectives agreed upon after extensive analysis, probing, and discussion by scholars, teachers, curriculum specialists, and laymen. The guiding principle for devising evaluation measures was to determine what an individual could be asked to do to indicate his attainment of the objective. While objective measures were most common, interviews, free responses, and questionnaires were also planned. In each situation a determined effort has been made to test the validity of the measures; in other words, to match the questions and exercises to the objectives they were designed to measure. Campbell and Nichols (46) throw some light on evaluation of objectives for citizenship; Kurfman (206) describes the evaluation of objectives in social studies.

An effort of a different sort has been directed toward evaluation of curriculum programs in social studies. Morrissett and Stevens (240) report on a promising effort by the staff of the Social Science Education Consortium. Members of this group, concerned about how to analyze an increasing number of curriculum materials being produced by various projects and publishing houses, created a curriculum analysis system for such purpose. Based upon two major sources of information—examination of materials and classroom experience—the analysis considers the following: descriptive characteristics, rationale, objectives, teacher capabilities and training, structure of the curriculum materials, teacher strategies and learning theory, and evaluation. In each category, attention is directed to specific aspects of the materials. The resulting data provide an informative and useful description of curriculum design.

Especially interesting is the requirement for the evaluation category (240: 486): "Analysis will establish the basis for formulating judgments, determining to what extent the general objectives and specific or behavioral objectives have been accomplished, and making explicit how we know they have been accomplished."

An interesting attempt to analyze an elementary social studies curriculum in terms of its provisions for the development of cognitive processes and skills was made by Biles (24). The curriculum plan, prepared by a Texas elementary school, was a series of depth studies based on California generalizations with emphasis upon cognitive processes. The researcher collected and analyzed the learning activities in terms of their success in clearly providing for development of cognitive skills and their progression in demand for higher skills from level to level. Biles concluded that the teachers had not been successful in designing the kind of course they had set out to plan.

Jarolimek (178), after surveying the current status of social studies in the elementary school, outlines 12 guidelines for assessing the elementary school social studies program. The guidelines as a whole offer criteria for curriculum evaluation, as reported in Chapter 2, and the twelfth guideline in particular asks, "Is it possible to evaluate the program in order to establish with some degree of confidence the extent to which major purposes have been achieved?" The answer to this question is the point of much that has been said in this chapter.

7. Teacher Education in Social Studies

TEACHER preparation must be considered an important facet of any study of research findings related to elementary school social studies. Although research pertaining specifically to this area is rather limited at the present, some valuable work which will serve as a basis for future development has been completed. In this section suggestions of authorities in the field will be included in the discussion.

Teacher Competencies in the Social Studies

A determination of teacher competencies in elementary school social studies would be of valuable assistance in identifying problems which might be overcome by certain modifications in preservice and in-service educational patterns. Certainly studies like the one by Herman (160), which indicates that pupils have little interest in social studies, and other studies, such as the one by DeWitt (79), which shows a considerable gap between theory and practice in relation to methods of teaching, emphasize the significance of the teacher's role. Numerous articles and somewhat fewer research studies regarding the relative strengths, weaknesses, and needs of these teachers have been reported recently in the literature.

That new programs in elementary social studies will necessitate a strengthening of teacher education programs is a point emphasized by Fraser (112). She notes that most social studies teachers now in service do not feel secure with the new content and methodology being introduced. She points out that most of these teachers have made little or no study of anthropology, sociology, or social psychology, and that their exposure to economics and geography has been limited. History and political science have been dominant in their preservice preparation. She recommends a strengthening of preservice preparation and a massive in-service study in the social sciences. Of equal importance is study related to learning materials.

Further evidence of inadequate teacher preparation in the social sciences is supplied by Hahn (145), who found that only three percent of the social studies teachers in elementary schools in Minnesota had taken college work in political science. Godwin (129) gave a discouraging report of his study of 190 Nebraska elementary teachers. He found that fewer than half had had recent instruction in social studies teaching or viewed social studies as experts do. In general, teachers were proceeding in a conventional way, treating social studies as a separate textbook subject. Similarly, Veltkamp (333) found teachers in the tri-state region of Iowa, Minnesota, and South Dakota to be poorly prepared to teach elementary geography.

Lack of competence in economics was borne out by a report of the National Task Force on Economic Education (90). The survey revealed evidence that social studies teachers, on the average, do not know much more than high school students about their economy and that in-service teachers who have recently taken work in economics do not do very well on even a relatively easy test of economic facts and principles. On the other hand, Chandler (51), after gathering grade point averages and administering the *Sequential Test of Educational Progress* and the *American College Test* to 417 juniors and seniors at the University of Tennessee, concluded that, in general, the elementary majors were qualified to teach social studies.

The Board of Directors of the National Council for the Social Studies in its guidelines of 1966 (143) also made recommendations regarding social studies teacher preparation. It recommended that the undergraduate do 25-30 percent of his course work in general education, 15-25 percent in professional education, and 50-60 percent in academic teaching fields. Elementary teachers should have a broad background in the social sciences, with course work in some depth relevant to their teaching areas.

Studies of problems encountered by beginning teachers of the social studies carry with them implications for improved teacher education. Wendt (341) conducted such a study using as subjects 147 elementary homeroom teachers engaged in teaching social studies in a large metropolitan area. Questionnaires, observations, and interviews revealed that backgrounds were limited and numerous problems were being encountered by the subjects. Problems noted in particular were these: finding reading material for children, helping children develop critical thinking skills, making full use of community resources, acquiring the social studies background for teaching units, helping children develop both independent study skills and group skills, organizing children in work groups, and organizing varied social studies learning experiences to meet the needs and interests of children. For assistance in improving instruction, the teachers preferred special workshops, development of new social studies guides, televised demonstrations of social studies lessons, observations of other teachers, and in-service courses. Wendt concluded with recommendations that school systems sponsor workshops, organize committees to study improvement possibilities, and provide televised demonstration lessons. She also recommended that universities reexamine their teacher preparatory programs and lend assistance to school systems in improving the teaching of social studies.

Schilson (284) also studied problems of 127 beginning teachers in elementary social studies. Questionnaires revealed that most of their problems occurred in these three general areas: texts, curriculum guides, and supplementary materials; audio-visual and other teaching aids; pupil interest, pupil participation, and teaching method. Questionnaires received from supervisors identified considerably fewer problems of beginning teachers than did the teachers themselves.

Inn (175) explored problems encountered by beginning teachers in implementing a concept-based social studies curriculum. By means of interviews, conferences, and written responses, data were obtained from 60 elementary school teachers in Hawaii. The chief difficulty encountered was the selection and implementation of relevant learning experiences for pupils. An analysis of this difficulty revealed these problems: The teachers' own grasp of the particular concept or generalization was critical. Appropriate learning activities were often overlooked because teachers did not realize that a conceptual objective itself may suggest suitable pupil experiences. In their search for the varied and unusual, the teachers often overlooked their major conceptual objective. The teachers' reliance on discussion throughout the development of the unit of study needed to be reevaluated.

Pendergast (247), studying changes in role perception, found that the beginning social studies teachers in the study held a rather tenuous commitment to their career and that the subjects of this inquiry had unclear definitions of their role. He recommended that greater emphasis be placed upon the identity of a professional commitment and the clarification of teacher roles early in the preservice training of teachers. To study teachers' perception of effective social studies teaching, Cannon (47) asked 50 experienced teachers their views on a good social studies program. Results of the survey indicated stress upon readiness, teacher-pupil planning, teacher appraisal as reinforcement, acquisition of knowledge, and the teaching of economic efficiency. One of the more disturbing studies of teacher competence, however, was designed by Weiser and Hayes (340). To examine the democratic attitudes of teachers and prospective teachers, they administered the *Purdue Opinion Poll* to students in the professional education sequence at Central Michigan College during the winter and spring of 1964-65. Practicing teachers were included also. The poll revealed that teachers generally expressed views that were not consistent with principles of democracy; results raised troublesome questions about how many teachers really understand democracy.

Two pieces of research in this area have an international flavor. Johnston (188) explored knowledge related to international understanding possessed by 300 teachers. He found that the following groups of people scored significantly higher on his measuring instrument: male teachers, teachers who had traveled outside the United States for at least three months, teachers with the greater amount of academic preparation, and teachers with more than 21 years of experience. Ninety-nine percent of the teachers felt that fostering international understanding is a responsibility of the teacher and the school.

Kranyik (203) directed his research more specifically to a comparison of the images of Mexican culture possessed by Connecticut and Mexican teachers and portrayed in certain elementary social studies textbooks. Results obtained from a questionnaire showed that the Connecticut teacher's image of Mexico differed significantly from the textbook image in 12 of the aspects. Furthermore, Connecticut and Mexican teacher images differed from each other in 9 of 16 cultural aspects.

Questions about teacher competency always give rise to problems of teacher selection. Lavender (209) attempted to find out whether or not superintendents could successfully select teachers through decisions based solely on credentials. He found, interestingly enough, that experienced superintendents could better anticipate successful teacher activities outside the classroom than successful teacher activities within.

As one of the major weaknesses in social studies programs, Bailey (15) cited the number of junior high school teachers assigned to teach subjects for which they were unprepared. Hansen

(149), in a survey of selected junior high schools in Wisconsin, found that 62 percent of the social studies teachers had neither a major nor a minor in any area of the social studies, that none of the teachers in the sample who had a major in history was assigned to teach history on a full-time basis, and that the most commonly taught units in the seventh and ninth grades were those for which teachers were least prepared in terms of academic background. On the other hand, Irvin (177), after a survey of junior high school social studies teachers in three North Central Region high schools, recommended that the total number of academic hours in social studies be reduced except for geography and that the time gained be given to study designed to help teachers meet the special problems of junior high school young people.

Preservice Education

A study of the sophisticated content and the inquiry-oriented methodologies associated with the various social studies projects under way makes apparent the necessity of quality teacher preparatory programs. A further study of the relative strengths and weaknesses of teachers already in service indicates that many preservice practices of the past are not adequate to the task.

Consider first the academic preparation of the prospective elementary school teacher. Although not directing his attention specifically to the social studies, Frazier (116) noted that contact with the academic areas in college has been insufficient to provide background for teaching today's children. The teacher has been placed in professional education so early in his college career that he comes back to college as a postgraduate unable to reenter the content sequences except at the undergraduate level. Hill (167) emphasized the importance of a broad liberal arts background in the areas of the social sciences, the humanities, and the sciences. More specifically, she recommended courses in geography, history, social science, economics, sociology, and anthropology for the prospective teacher of social studies in the elementary school.

White (345) directed his attention to social studies in a study of selected teacher education institutions in Tennessee. He found that the state's requirements were met or exceeded by each of the selected institutions in all areas compared. None of the institutions, however, met all of the recommendations of the National Council for the Social Studies, the deficiencies occurring in the areas of general education and social studies endorsement.

Very little has been done to the present time in structuring content courses in the social studies in terms of the background and needs of prospective teachers. One such effort in economics, however, is an example. Motivated by the findings of the National Task Force on Economic Education, cited earlier in this chapter, faculty of the Carnegie Institute of Technology (280) designed a new, one-semester course required of all sophomores, a course designed to do a few things well rather than to attempt to cover the field. While carefully structured to develop an interest in and an acquaintance with basic economics, the course did not succeed in developing students' ability to transfer knowledge to practical problems. The directors of the study concluded that teachers must have repeated experiences with such transfer in a variety of situations if they are to be able to use this skill.

The professional education of the social studies teacher has also come under recent scrutiny. A general pattern of dissatisfaction with the status quo is giving impetus to studies to identify specific problem areas, suggestions to improve the situation, subsequent testing of these suggestions, and ultimately to the assimilation of the innovations into existing programs. Typical of statements of discontent is this one by Metcalf (232: 200): "The methods course is under heavy fire. Unless it is revolutionized, it will probably be abolished."

McAulay (228) undertook a study to determine how the methods course in the social studies was perceived by teachers. Interviews with 64 first-year teachers from 17 colleges resulted in the following: Teachers said that the courses had provided little or no opportunity for observing the methods and techniques being described. Teachers found that they had been inadequately prepared in the area of organizing for instruction. They made recommendations regarding grade-level emphasis in methods classes, feeling that there was too little attention given to the primary level. They expressed a need also for a current events unit in methods. Finally, teachers commented that they wanted to be tested and evaluated in the social studies methods course as they would be expected to test and evaluate their pupils. It might be concluded that methods courses verbalize too much and demonstrate too little.

Smith (304) administered a questionnaire to 78 first-semester senior elementary majors who were taking methods courses prior to student teaching. Eighty-seven percent of the students indicated they would have taken methods courses whether they were required or not. Ninety-one percent expressed the opinion that the methods course should be required for certification. The students felt that methods courses were a useful preparation for teaching.

On the other hand, an analysis by Monson (237) of programs of Utah universities and colleges preparing elementary teachers in social studies produced evidence that those enrolling in the courses generally rated them of moderate to little help in preparing for teaching. Unit structure and critical thinking were given most emphasis in the methods courses; history, psychology, and geography were the most prominent subjects in academic preparation.

Numerous proposals for the improvement of teacher education have been made. Research and development related to the feasibility of various of these proposals are becoming increasingly more prevalent.

The use of television is an example of such a proposal. Although using a limited sample in his study, Chabe (50) found that observation by closed-circuit television in elementary social studies methods courses was almost as effective as observation in actual classrooms. He did recommend, however, that any such viewing be conducted on a guided basis. In an introductory course in secondary education, Adolphsen (3) found that the nature of observational experiences, rather than the media, was the significant factor in differentiating the perception of teacher behavior. Gross and McCormac (142) have reported on rather promising work being done at the Stanford Center for Research and Development in Teaching, under a grant from the U.S. Office of Education. Those involved in social studies teacher education at Stanford have used video tapes in an effort to maximize television as a facilitator of instruction. At the time of the reporting, the program directors were in the process of developing tapes in actual classrooms to demonstrate the types of behavior and situations being described to students in teacher education classes. They point out that among the many advantages of video tape are its flexibility in length and viewing audience and its ability to provide the methods class with concrete illustrations of both good and poor performances, a variety of teaching environments, and differing teaching techniques.

The INSITE Project (176), inaugurated at Indiana University and funded through the Ford Foundation, developed an innovative, comprehensive program of teacher education, one facet of which pertained to the preparation of teachers of social studies in the elementary school. This facet of the program was so designed that the students involved in the project took their methods course simultaneously with student teaching, the methodological emphasis being heavier at the beginning and then phasing out with full-time student teaching ultimately replacing it as the focal point. A cohesive, integrated experience was produced as the methods topics were actually related to student experiences in the classroom, as the students viewed their own performances as well as demonstration lessons on video tape, and as the college faculty and the cooperating teachers worked together as a team to help the student teacher during his student teaching experience.

Teachers of social studies have a direct responsibility and a specific role in educating the children of the poor. Frazier (115), for example, cited some findings of Project Aware, a nationwide research project to assess the preparation of school personnel for working with disadvantaged children and youth. Data revealed that, of the colleges which incorporated some type of preparation in this area, 60 percent reported accomplishing their goals through the modification of existing courses in methodology and in curriculum and organization and through such newly required courses as urban sociology, educational sociology, anthropology, and community psychology. It is apparent that work in the social sciences is considered important for teachers involved in teaching the disadvantaged.

Much of the research cited thus far has depended heavily upon interviews and questionnaires. Although this type of research produces useful, informative results, it does not tap the full range of knowledge obtainable. Promising results are being obtained from work designed to describe and to classify objectively various aspects of the teaching process. Obviously, not all of the research has been directed specifically to the area of social studies teacher preparation, but the techniques and devices being developed can readily be applied to the area. Work by Flanders (104) in interaction analysis, for example, has been vital to the area of teacher behavior.

Other research dealing with the development of ways to classify and analyze teacher behavior has been reported by Schueler, Gold, and Mitzel (289) and Turner and Fattu (330). These represent only a sampling of studies which hold promise for future work in elementary social studies teacher preparation.

In-Service Education

Although improvements in preservice education are encouraging, they are still not adequate if the implementation of the "new" social studies is to be fully realized. In-service education is needed if the desired changes are to be effected quickly, comprehensively, and in a satisfactory manner.

That until recently social studies have taken a subordinate position in the hierarchy of topics being stressed for in-service work was quite apparent in an article by Miel (233). She reported that an examination of articles listed under the heading "Institutes" in the *Education Index* during the period from 1950 through 1966 revealed social studies to be lagging behind every other topic in total number of reported institutes on in-service education. A questionnaire provided additional information. One hundred fifty-nine usable replies received from directors and supervisors of elementary education throughout the country reported on nearly 72,000 teachers. In the section of the index dealing with subject areas currently receiving particular emphasis in in-service programs, social studies ranked fourth. It also was listed fourth in terms of the number of teachers attending institutes on college campuses. On the other hand, public school systems across the country are not unmindful of the importance of supporting the ideals of professional growth and development. A survey of 334 school systems made in 1965-66 by the National Education Association Research Division (258) revealed a great variety of activities accepted as fulfilling professional growth requirements in these schools.

Independent research in in-service education in elementary social studies has been sparse. Most research has appeared as doctoral dissertations. In a study involving 14 teachers in self-contained fifth-grade social studies classrooms, Schreiber (288) found that the types of questions asked by teachers varied from one lesson to another and that a brief instructional program designed to improve the teachers' question-asking techniques did, in fact, modify their question-asking practices. Crump (68) found that programmed instruction in the art of questioning in social studies improved teacher questioning behavior in both social studies discussion and test construction. Her study also confirmed the fact that teachers normally use fact-seeking questions a great proportion of the time in discussion and testing and often impede the discussion process by poor questioning habits. Gagnon (118) discovered that training in the methodology of question-asking changed teachers' behavior to such an extent that when compared to untrained teachers they used five times as many clarifying questions and that their pupils showed a significantly larger number of "thought indicators." Davis and Tinsley (77) found that the questions asked by student teachers were largely of the memory-comprehension type with little stimulus to divergency. He strongly recommended that specific attention to the process of questioning be included in the preservice experiences of teachers.

Lea (210) conducted a questionnaire study of the methods and materials used by social studies teachers. She analyzed teacher responses in terms of the amount and variety of reading materials they used in the classroom. The teachers who used more materials also made more extensive use of unit planning, had had longer student teaching experiences, and had received more in-service training. Brandt (31) developed and evaluated an in-service education program for first-grade teachers involved in an experimental social studies and science project designed to promote concept and language development in disadvantaged Mexican-American children. The basic assumption of Brandt's study was that the achievement of children who were taught by teachers who had had significant in-service education would be greater than the achievement of children who were taught by teachers without such a program. The findings did not entirely support this assumption. Pankey (246) found that in-service education, in the form of an economic education workshop, made no significant difference in the economics understanding of a group of West Virginia teachers.

Recommendations for in-service education in social studies should be noted. Frazier (116) recommended a more comprehensive program of advanced education and more opportunity for subject specialization. After analyzing the activities and verbal behavior of selected fifth-grade social studies classes, Herman (158) recommended that in-service workshops on verbal behavior be expanded to enable teachers to learn a verbal interaction-analysis system and that in-service meetings relate characteristics of children to social studies instruction. Taba (322) emphasized the importance of inductive teaching as a prerequisite for inductive learning and identified in-service education not as a remedial technique but as an agent of change. Wendt's (341) study confirmed teachers' desire for creative in-service opportunities. A model for an in-service education program described by Schomburg (287) emphasizes eight elements: context (expectations of the population being serviced); input (teacher knowledge of the needs of pupils); selection of content; teaching strategies; selection of instructional materials; sequenced learning experiences; evaluational diagnosis; and feedback. He places emphasis upon involvement of the teacher through demonstration teaching, micro-teaching, and interaction analysis.

Institutes, workshops, and government-supported graduate programs have been reported in the literature. Westin and Smith (344) have described in detail the work at the Center for Research and Education in American Liberties, which was created as a joint project of Columbia University and Teachers College. Among the many activities of the center was the development of an institute model designed to improve the teaching about liberty. Ellsworth and Allen (93) described a two-week summer program for social studies teachers held annually in Detroit, Michigan, in cooperation with various local civic groups. At the university level the U.S. Office of Education has approved Experienced Teacher Fellowship programs in the social sciences (96).

A particularly exciting project begun under the Experienced Teacher Fellowship program was the establishment of Chicago's Center for Inner City Studies, a branch of Northeastern Illinois State College (315). Working together in the center are creative faculty and students determined to exemplify how community and university can work together to remake inner city education. Students who have received special instruction in research have produced original studies in communication, local history, and programmed instruction. Inner city problems and minority cultures receive special emphasis. One of the major goals is to "help participants put their stereotypes, fears, and prejudices against minorities in better balance with the realities of human differences and similarities" (315: 531).

Unfortunately, not all programs are as dynamic as this Chicago one. It is becoming apparent that certain government-sponsored programs which stressed courses and seminars are giving way to support of programs like the Tri-University Project which puts its emphasis upon teacher performance rather than on knowledge acquired through formal instruction. Jarolimek and others (180) have described several aspects of the Tri-University Project in Social Studies, based at the University of Washington. Kaltsounis (198) discusses a variety of efforts to improve teacher behavior in the social studies, including the idea of the in-service "sabbatical."

The various social studies projects described in an earlier chapter are making valuable contributions to in-service education. It was realized quite early in program development that teacher preparation would be essential if the projects were to proceed satisfactorily. The preparatory work has taken many forms. Fenton and Good (101), in a progress report on Project Social Studies, noted that some projects involve the classroom teachers in actually developing materials; others have them plan teaching strategies, while still others have them try out materials and report their findings. Revisions are made on the basis of teacher reports.

Illustrative of in-service practices is work being done on projects at the University of Minnesota and the University of Georgia. In describing the project at the University of Minnesota, West (343) noted that teachers' institutes had been held to train teachers to use the new materials and that staff members had worked with teachers in the field and revised materials in the light of teacher reactions.

Rice and Bailey (266) reported that each experimental school associated with the project at the University of Georgia has had two types of cooperating teachers at each grade level: an experimental teacher who receives training in anthropology and a control teacher who also uses the materials but does not have training in anthropology. This arrangement permits the project to determine the instructional utility of the materials produced for the general elementary teacher who has had no training in anthropology. In a study based on this same project, Greene (140) found that there were no significant differences in achievement favoring pupils taught by teachers who had had experience with the anthropology materials prior to their work with children.

The Greater Cleveland Social Science Program (73; 134) also has been engaged in a rather extensive in-service education project. An innovative and highly successful educative practice was the use of telelectures. A closed-circuit telephone network was established so that many teachers could hear outstanding speakers in the social sciences and then could question them directly following their lectures. A series of 12 tapes has been made of the telelectures. Independent study materials have also been developed to aid the teacher in his learning.

In a government-funded project, Harnack (152) has developed a unique in-service program. An electronic computer delivers to teachers suggested group and individual unit activities in social studies when teachers submit to the computer center objectives selected from a master file and a check list of pupil characteristics. Implementation of the suggestions, of course, rests with the teachers, but making such resources almost instantly available has in-service possibilities of some magnitude.

The importance of teacher education in social studies, both preservice and in-service, can hardly be overemphasized. For the findings of research and developmental work to be of maximum value in the classroom, the teacher must be confident and secure with regard to process and to content. Efforts to date have revealed a growing interest on the part of teachers and a promising measure of success in the formulative stages of innovative programs devoted to the preparation of social studies teachers.

Conclusion

RESEARCH in elementary social studies is continuing apace. While the studies of the decade just past have added much to the knowledge of what to teach and how to teach, there are many unanswered questions. Perhaps in no other area of the elementary school are there more basic problems to be solved and more opportunities for definitive research.

Price and others (255), reporting the proceedings of a conference devoted to exploring needed research in social studies, raised again some of the perennial questions: In the realm of objectives, what shall be taught? Facts? Methods? Values? Beliefs? Shall learning be guided by principles of maturation or by the concept of early introduction of concepts? What factors determine when something may be learned most efficiently and effectively? What kinds of content stimulate curiosity and at what levels? Is there one method or several? How do various approaches influence beliefs, attitudes, and values? Under what conditions does commitment lead to actions?

Problems of a different nature are posed when social studies educators consider the current social scene. What should the school teach about war, population growth, pollution, prejudice? How can pupils be prepared for participation in a world fighting for its survival? How can social studies challenge boys and girls to courageous action for the future? What kind of social studies is best suited to pupils of the inner city? How can social studies contribute to better human relationships? How can social studies become more relevant to real life? These concerns are urgent and profound.

In pondering unsolved problems and unanswered questions against the backdrop of the research reviewed in this booklet, the reader senses that—in spite of its quantity—much of it has been scattered and piecemeal. A pressing need now is to find a way to select the best of the pieces, to fit them together into meaningful models, and to test the application of such models to social studies instruction.

The difficulty of accomplishing the organization of what is

already known is truly monumental. As yet there have been only a very few efforts to promote communication among those carrying on research and those who are ready to test innovations. A national clearinghouse is desperately needed—an agency that can gather, sort, evaluate, and publish the research that will most likely cast light on existing problems in social studies education. Furthermore, ways must be found to disseminate the results of many doctoral dissertations which at present are readily available only in brief abstracts. Encouraging these investigators to describe their studies in widely-used periodicals would be helpful. Replication of the best of all the available research in a variety of locales and with pupils of differing capabilities and backgrounds would in time produce reliable evidence upon which to build new programs.

The past decade has witnessed the birth of the "new" social studies. The months ahead afford opportunities for extension, variation, and refinement. Unusual and profitable beginnings have been made; directions for the future are taking shape.

Bibliography

1. JOHN QUINCY ADAMS, JR. "Selected Variables Related to the Frequency of Questions Asked in Social Studies in Grades Five and Six." Doctor's Dissertation, Arizona State University, 1961. *Dissertation Abstracts* 24: 192; July 1963.

2. THOMAS HOWARD ADAMS. "The Development of a Method for Analysis of Questions Asked by Teachers in Classroom Discussion." Doctor's Dissertation, Rutgers, The State University, 1964. *Dissertation Abstracts* 25: 2809-10; November 1964.

3. LOUIS JOHN ADOLPHSEN. "A Comparison of the Effectiveness of Selected Observational Procedures in Developing Teacher Perceptions." Doctor's Dissertation, University of Minnesota, 1961. *Dissertation Abstracts* 22: 3933-34; May 1962.

4. SAAD MORSI AHMED. "A Survey of Curriculum Materials in Some Selected School Systems as They Relate to Education for International Understanding." Doctor's Dissertation, Indiana University, 1962. *Dissertation Abstracts* 27: 1290A-91A; November 1966.

5. NANCY JEAN ALLBAUGH. "Comprehension of Three Levels of Social Studies Material as Designated by a Readability Formula." Doctor's Dissertation, The University of Iowa, 1968. *Dissertation Abstracts* 29: 1665A; December 1968.

6. DWIGHT WILLIAM ALLEN. "Evaluation in Social Studies Classrooms: Ideals and Practices." Doctor's Dissertation, Stanford University, 1959. *Dissertation Abstracts* 20: 1282-83; October 1959.

7. ARTHUR LEROY ANDERSON. "An Investigation of Sources of Collateral Reading To Enrich Social Studies Units Taught in the Elementary School." Doctor's Dissertation, Colorado State College, 1966. *Dissertation Abstracts* 27: 2093A; January 1967.

8. MELVIN ARNOFF. "Adding Depth to Elementary School Social Studies." *Social Education* 28: 335-36; October 1964.

9. MELVIN ARNOFF. *The Development of First Grade Materials on "Families of Japan."* USOE Project 5-8070. (ERIC ED 010 339) Kent, Ohio: Kent State University.

10. VAL E. ARNSDORF. "An Investigation of the Teaching of Chronology in the Sixth Grade." *Journal of Experimental Education* 29: 307-13; March 1961.

11. VAL E. ARNSDORF. "A Study of Intermediate Grade Children's Understanding of Basal Social Studies Materials." *California Journal of Educational Research* 14: 67-73; January 1963.

94   ELEMENTARY SCHOOL SOCIAL STUDIES

12. VAL E. ARNSDORF. "Readability of Basal Social Studies Materials." *The Reading Teacher* 16: 243-46; January 1963.

13. VAL E. ARNSDORF. "Teaching Map-Reading and Geographic Understandings with Projectuals." *Journal of Geography* 63: 75-81; February 1964.

14. VAL E. ARNSDORF. "Time and Space Terms in Basal Social Studies Materials." *California Journal of Educational Research* 14: 23-29; January 1963.

15. GEORGE WARD BAILEY. "Problems and Trends in Junior High School Social Studies." Doctor's Dissertation, The University of Nebraska Teachers College, 1964. *Dissertation Abstracts* 25: 177-78; July 1964.

16. WILFRED BAILEY and MARION J. RICE. *Development of a Sequential Curriculum in Anthropology for Grades 1-7.* USOE Project 5-1024. (ERIC ED 011 209) Athens, Georgia: University of Georgia.

17. EUGENE HAROLD BAKER. "A Comparison Study of Textbook and Simulation Approaches in Teaching Junior High School American History." Doctor's Dissertation, Northwestern University, 1966. *Dissertation Abstracts* 27: 3353A-54A; April 1967.

18. JAMES A. BANKS. "A Content Analysis of the Black American in Textbooks." *Social Education* 33: 954-57, 963; December 1969.

19. JAMES A. BANKS. "Relevant Social Studies for Black Pupils." *Social Education* 33: 66-69; January 1969.

20. EDWARD WILLIAM BEAUBIER. "Capacity of Sixth Grade Children To Understand Social Science Generalizations." Doctor's Dissertation, University of Southern California, 1962. *Dissertation Abstracts* 23: 2439-40; January 1963.

21. LORETTA ELAINE BELGUM. "An Investigation of the Effect of Teaching Interpretation of Geographic Photographs to Sixth Graders." Doctor's Dissertation, University of California at Berkeley, 1967. *Dissertation Abstracts* 29: 53A; July 1968.

22. JAMES RICHARD BEMIS. "Geography in the Elementary School Social Studies Program." Doctor's Dissertation, University of Southern California, 1966. *Dissertation Abstracts* 27: 989A-90A; October 1966.

23. HARRY D. BERG, editor. *Evaluation in Social Studies.* Thirty-Fifth Yearbook. Washington, D.C.: National Council for the Social Studies, 1965. 251 pp.

24. RAYMOND EMMETT BILES. "An Analysis of an Elementary Social Studies Program, 1963-64: Provisions for the Development of Cognitive Processes and Skills." Doctor's Dissertation, The University of Texas, 1967. *Dissertation Abstracts* 28: 1609A-10A; November 1967.

25. GLEN MYERS BLAIR, R. STEWART JONES, and RAY H. SIMPSON. *Educational Psychology.* New York: The Macmillan Company, 1962. 678 pp.

26. STANLEY SOLOMON BLANK. "Inquiry Training Through Programmed Instruction." Doctor's Dissertation, University of California at Berkeley, 1963. *Dissertation Abstracts* 24: 1071; September 1963.

27. ELAINE CARLIN BLOCK. "Sequence as a Factor in Classroom

Instruction." Doctor's Dissertation, The University of Wisconsin, 1965. *Dissertation Abstracts* 25: 5778-79; April 1965.

28. BENJAMIN S. BLOOM. *Taxonomy of Educational Objectives: Handbook I, Cognitive Domain.* New York: David McKay Company, Inc., 1956. 207 pp.

29. SARANE S. BOOCOCK. "An Experimental Study of the Learning Effects of Two Games with Simulated Environments." *American Behavioral Scientist* 10: 8-17; October 1966.

30. NORMAN EDWARD BOTTORFF. "The Reaction of Third Grade Low and Middle Class Children to Selected Social Studies Words." Doctor's Dissertation, The Pennsylvania State University, 1966. *Dissertation Abstracts* 27: 2932A-33A; March 1967.

31. DOROTHY PAULINE BRANDT. "The Development and Evaluation of an In-Service Program in Social Studies and Science for First-Grade Teachers." Doctor's Dissertation, The University of Texas, 1967. *Dissertation Abstracts* 28: 4021A; April 1968.

32. LESLIE J. BRIGGS. "Learner Variables and Educational Media." *Review of Educational Research* 38: 160-76; April 1968.

33. DANIEL H. BROWN. "Knowledge of Important Principles of Physical Geography Possessed by Selected Sixth-Grade Children." Doctor's Dissertation, University of Kansas, 1963. *Dissertation Abstracts* 24: 5072-73; June 1964.

34. HAROLD JESS BROWN. "The Construction and Standardization of a Concept Prerequisite and Development Test." Doctor's Dissertation, Utah State University, 1965. *Dissertation Abstracts* 29: 178A-79A; June 1968.

35. HELEN BROWN. "Basic Economic Concepts Taught in Public Elementary Schools of Louisiana, 1967-1968." Doctor's Dissertation, Louisiana State University and Agricultural and Mechanical College, 1968. *Dissertation Abstracts* 29: 1354A; November 1968.

36. ROBERT BROWN. *CUE (Culture, Understanding, Enrichment) Social Studies.* Project NDEA-VIIB-324-2. New York: New York State Department of Education.

37. JEROME S. BRUNER. "Man: A Course of Study." *ESI Quarterly Report.* Watertown, Massachusetts: Educational Services, Inc. (Now Education Development Center.) Summer-Fall 1965. pp. 85-95.

38. JEROME S. BRUNER. "Structures in Learning." *Today's Education* (formerly *NEA Journal*) 52: 26-27; March 1963.

39. JEROME S. BRUNER. *Toward a Theory of Instruction.* Cambridge, Massachusetts: Harvard University Press, 1966. 176 pp.

40. DOROTHY M. BRYAN. "Education for the Culturally Deprived: Building on Pupil Experience." *Social Education* 31: 117-18; February 1967.

41. RICHARD DALE BUCKLEY. "A Comparison of Set Diagrams and Lists as Aids in Learning Relationships in Social Studies." Doctor's Dissertation, University of Pittsburgh, 1967. *Dissertation Abstracts* 28: 3547A; March 1968.

96   ELEMENTARY SCHOOL SOCIAL STUDIES

42. BRUCE B. BURNES and GORDON E. HERSHBERGER. "Involving Graduate Students in Curriculum: The Adams-Morgan Project." *Educational Leadership* 26: 151-53; November 1968.

43. GLORIA CAMMAROTA. "Children, Politics, and Elementary Social Studies." *Social Education* 27: 205-207, 211; April 1963.

44. GLORIA CAMMAROTA. "New Emphases in Social Studies for the Primary Grades." *Social Education* 27: 77-80; February 1963.

45. VINCENT N. CAMPBELL. *Degree of Student Control over Programmed Instruction: Cumulative Effects on Problem Solving and Transfer.* Cooperative Research Project C-998. (ERIC ED 003 218) American Institute for Research in Behavioral Sciences.

46. VINCENT N. CAMPBELL and DARYL G. NICHOLS. "National Assessment of Citizenship Education." *Social Education* 32: 279-81; March 1968.

47. FRANCES OWENS CANNON. "Teacher Perceptions of Successful Teaching of Social Studies in the Elementary School Curriculum." Doctor's Dissertation, University of Alabama, 1966. *Dissertation Abstracts* 27: 598A; September 1966.

48. DENNIS R. CARMICHAEL. "Developing Map Reading Skills and Geographic Understandings by Means of Conceptual Teaching Methods." Doctor's Dissertation, University of California at Berkeley, 1965. *Dissertation Abstracts* 26: 7176; June 1966.

49. RONALD JOHN BERRY CARSWELL. "Topographic Map Reading Abilities of Learners in Grade Four, Five and Six." Doctor's Dissertation, The University of Florida, 1968. *Dissertation Abstracts* 30: 200A; July 1969.

50. ALEXANDER M. CHABE. "Experiment with CCTV in Teacher Education." *Peabody Journal of Education* 40: 24-30; July 1962.

51. JOSEPH DOUGLAS CHANDLER. "An Analysis of Competence in the Social Sciences by Elementary Education Majors at the University of Tennessee." Doctor's Dissertation, The University of Tennessee, 1966. *Dissertation Abstracts* 27: 3246A-47A; April 1967.

52. W. LINWOOD CHASE. "American History in the Middle Grades." In: William Cartwright and Richard L. Watson, Jr., editors. *Interpreting and Teaching American History.* Thirty-First Yearbook, Washington, D.C.: National Council for the Social Studies, 1961. pp. 329-43.

53. C. I. CHATTO and A. L. HALLIGAN. *The Story of the Springfield Plan.* New York: Barnes & Noble, Inc., 1945. 201 pp.

54. CLEO H. CHERRYHOLMES. "Some Current Research on Effectiveness of Educational Simulations: Implications for Alternative Strategies." *American Behavioral Scientist* 10: 4-7; October 1966.

55. VICTORIA CHEW. "Social Science Generalizations in Selected Second-Grade Textbooks." Doctor's Dissertation, The University of California at Berkeley, 1966. *Dissertation Abstracts* 27: 2438A; February 1967.

56. H. MILLARD CLEMENTS, WILLIAM R. FIELDER, and B. ROBERT

TABACHNICK. *Social Study: Inquiry in Elementary Classrooms.* Indianapolis: Bobbs-Merrill Company, Inc., 1966. 402 pp.

57. *A Conceptual Framework for the Social Studies in Wisconsin Schools.* Madison, Wisconsin: Wisconsin Department of Public Instruction, 1964. 37 pp.

58. ROBERT L. CORNISH. "Suggestions for Improving the Social Studies." *Peabody Journal of Education* 44: 223-29; January 1967.

59. *Course of Study for Virginia Elementary Schools.* Richmond, Virginia: State Board of Education, 1943. 553 pp.

60. CHARLOTTE ANTOINETTE CRABTREE. "Effects of Structuring on Productiveness of Children's Thinking: A Study of Second Grade Dramatic Play Patterns Centered in Harbor and Airport Activities Under Two Types of Teacher Structuring." Doctor's Dissertation, Stanford University, 1962. *Dissertation Abstracts* 23: 161; July 1962.

61. CHARLOTTE A. CRABTREE. "Inquiry Approaches: How New and How Valuable?" *Social Education* 30: 523-25, 531; November 1966.

62. CHARLOTTE A. CRABTREE. "Inquiry Approaches to Learning Concepts and Generalizations in Social Studies." *Social Education* 30: 407-11, 414; October 1966.

63. CHARLOTTE A. CRABTREE. *Teaching Geography in Grades One Through Three: Effects of Instruction in the Core Concept of Geographic Theory.* USOE Project 5-1037. Los Angeles: University of California at Los Angeles.

64. *Creativity in Urban Education.* Chicago: The Research Council of the Great Cities Program for School Improvement, 1968. 257 pp.

65. VINCENT ANTHONY CRISTIANI. "Informal Dramatization in Social Studies, Grade VI." Doctor's Dissertation, Boston University School of Education, 1960. *Dissertation Abstracts* 21: 3375; May 1961.

66. MURIEL CROSBY. *An Adventure in Human Relations: The Wilmington Story.* Chicago: Follett Publishing Company, 1965. 396 pp.

67. MURIEL CROSBY. "The Community and Its Schools: An Adventure in Human Relations." *Children* 11: 8-12; January-February 1964.

68. CLAUDIA CRUMP. "Self-Instruction in the Art of Questioning in Intermediate-Grade Social Studies." Doctor's Dissertation, Indiana University, 1969. 130 pp. Also see: Claudia Crump. "Teachers, Questions, and Cognition." *Educational Leadership* 27: 657-60; April 1970.

69. ROBERT L. CURRY. "Subject Preferences of Fifth-Grade Children." *Peabody Journal of Education* 41: 23-27; July 1963.

70. GARNEY LEWIS DARRIN. "Economics in the Elementary School Curriculum: A Study of the District of Columbia Laboratory Schools." Doctor's Dissertation, University of Maryland, 1959. *Dissertation Abstracts* 21: 95-96; July 1960.

71. DAVID WARREN DAVID. "Conditions That Foster Growth in Children's Ability To Generalize in Elementary School Social Studies."

Doctor's Dissertation, Indiana University, 1968. *Dissertation Abstracts* 29: 1805A; December 1968.

72. GORDON FRANCIS DAVIES. "Map Skills and Understandings in Intermediate School Social Studies." Doctor's Dissertation, Stanford University, 1962. *Dissertation Abstracts* 23: 948-49; September 1962.

73. HAROLD S. DAVIS. "New Approach to In-Service Education." *Educational Screen and Audiovisual Guide* 45: 28-29; May 1966.

74. JOHN EDWIN DAVIS. "The Ability of Fourth, Fifth, and Sixth Grade Pupils To Distinguish Between Fact and Opinion in an Experimentally Designed Reading Situation." Doctor's Dissertation, University of Oregon, 1964. *Dissertation Abstracts* 25: 1781; September 1964.

75. O. L. DAVIS, JR. "Learning About Time Zones in Grades Four, Five, and Six." *The Journal of Experimental Education* 31: 407-12; Summer 1963.

76. O. L. DAVIS, JR., and FRANCIS P. HUNKINS. "Textbook Questions: What Thinking Processes Do They Foster?" *Peabody Journal of Education* 43: 285-92; March 1966.

77. O. L. DAVIS, JR., and DREW C. TINSLEY. "Cognitive Objectives Revealed by Classroom Questions Asked by Social Studies Student Teachers." *Peabody Journal of Education* 45: 21-26; July 1967.

78. DOROTHY ANNABELLE DEBOER. "Concepts Basic to an Understanding of Alaska (Volumes I and II)." Doctor's Dissertation, Colorado State College, 1967. *Dissertation Abstracts* 28: 2886A-87A; February 1968.

79. CHARLES MAURICE DEWITT. "The Extent of the Relationship Between Theory and Practice in the Teaching of Social Studies in the Elementary School." Doctor's Dissertation, University of Maryland, 1957. *Dissertation Abstracts* 18: 522; February 1958.

80. DON C. DINKMEYER and RUDOLPH DREIKURS. *Encouraging Children To Learn.* Englewood Cliffs, New Jersey: Prentice-Hall, Inc., 1963. 162 pp.

81. *Directory of Research in Social Studies/Social Sciences.* USOE Bureau of Research Bulletin OE-31010. Washington, D.C.: U.S. Department of Health, Education, and Welfare, U.S. Office of Education, 1969. 27 pp.

82. EDITH LORRAINE DOBBS. "A Study of the Sequential Development of Time Sense and Chronology in the Elementary School." Doctor's Dissertation, University of Kansas, 1963. *Dissertation Abstracts* 24: 5075; June 1964.

83. ROBERT V. DUFFEY. "Practices Reported by Teachers in Elementary School Social Studies." In: Wayne L. Herman, Jr., editor. *Current Research in Elementary School Social Studies.* New York: The Macmillan Company, 1969. pp. 234-46.

84. DAVID GEOFFREY DUFTY. "Folksongs in the Social Studies in the United States and Australia: An Exploratory Study." Doctor's Dissertation, Stanford University, 1966. *Dissertation Abstracts* 27: 137A; July 1966.

85. MIRIAM CAIN DUSENBERRY. "Analysis of Selected Features of Older and Newer Editions of Certain Revisions of Fourth, Fifth, and Sixth Grade Social Studies Textbooks." Doctor's Dissertation, State University of Iowa, 1964. *Dissertation Abstracts* 25: 932-33; August 1964.

86. CHARLES ROBERT DuVALL. "Agreement of Judgments of Elementary Teachers and Measured Readability Level of Selected Free and Inexpensive Social Studies Materials." Doctor's Dissertation, Ohio University, 1966. *Dissertation Abstracts* 27: 2275A; February 1967.

87. CHARLES EDWARD DWYER. "Explorations of a Rational Method for Ethical Inquiry." Doctor's Dissertation, Cornell University, 1966. *Dissertation Abstracts* 27: 1292A-93A; November 1966.

88. DAVID EASTON and JACK DENNIS. "The Child's Image of Government." *The Annals of the American Academy of Political and Social Science* 361: 40-57; September 1965.

89. DAVID EASTON and ROBERT D. HESS. "The Child's Political World." *Midwest Journal of Political Science* 6: 229-46; August 1962.

90. *Economic Education in the Schools: A Report of the National Task Force on Economic Education.* New York: Committee for Economic Development, 1961. Available from the Joint Council on Economic Education. 78 pp.

91. ROBERT W. EDGAR. "History, Reading, and Human Relations: An Integrated Approach." *Social Education* 29: 155-58, 163; March 1965.

92. Educational Policies Commission. *The Central Purpose of American Education.* Washington, D.C.: National Education Association, 1961. 21 pp.

93. RUTH ELLSWORTH and ARTHUR T. ALLEN. "Teachers Study the Social Education of Urban Children." *The Elementary School Journal* 64: 420-26; May 1964.

94. RAYMOND ENGLISH. *The Greater Cleveland Social Science Program (K-12).* Cleveland, Ohio: Educational Research Council of Greater Cleveland.

95. FRANK J. ESTVAN and ELIZABETH W. ESTVAN. *The Child's World: His Social Perception.* New York: G. P. Putnam's Sons, 1959. 302 pp.

96. "Experienced Teacher Fellowship Programs in the Social Sciences: 1967-68." *Social Education* 31: 243; March 1967.

97. VERNA S. FANCETT and others. *Social Science Concepts and the Classroom.* Syracuse, New York: Social Studies Curriculum Center, Syracuse University, 1968. 64 pp.

98. IRVIN JOSEPH FARBER. "A Study of the Use of Programed Instruction in a Group Situation." Doctor's Dissertation, Temple University, 1965. *Dissertation Abstracts* 26: 1509-10; September 1965.

99. CHARLES ROBERT FARRAR. "Map Skills and Understandings in Upper Elementary School Social Studies." Doctor's Dissertation, Stanford University, 1963. *Dissertation Abstracts* 24: 1094-95; September 1963.

100. EDWIN FENTON. *The New Social Studies.* New York: Holt, Rinehart and Winston, Inc., 1967. 144 pp.

101. EDWIN FENTON and JOHN M. GOOD. "Project Social Studies: A Progress Report." *Social Education* 29: 206-208; April 1965.

102. HOWARD GEORGE FIELD. "A Study of Individual Differences of First and Second Grade Children's Ability To Recognize Concepts of Selected Second Grade Social Studies Content." Doctor's Dissertation, University of South Dakota, 1967. *Dissertation Abstracts* 28: 1615A-16A; November 1967.

103. FRANK L. FISHER. "Influences of Reading and Discussion on the Attitudes of Fifth Graders Toward American Indians." *The Journal of Educational Research* 62: 130-34; November 1968.

104. NED A. FLANDERS. *Teacher Influence, Pupil Attitudes, and Achievement.* USOE Cooperative Research Project 397. (ERIC ED 002 865) Minneapolis, Minnesota: University of Minnesota College of Education, 1960.

105. WILLIAM D. FLOYD. "Do Teachers Talk Too Much?" *The Instructor* 78: 53, 150; October 1968.

106. "Foreign Policy Association Bibliography on Simulation." *Social Education* 33: 195-99; February 1969.

107. EDITH C. FORSTER. "An Evaluation of the Field Trip in the Formation of Social Concepts and Generalizations." Doctor's Dissertation, Wayne State University, 1960. *Dissertation Abstracts* 22: 181; July 1961.

108. LILLIAN FINE FORTESS. "A Suggested Guide to the Use of Paintings as Resources in the Social Studies for the Middle Grades." Doctor's Dissertation, New York University, 1959. *Dissertation Abstracts* 20: 3998; April 1960.

109. ROBERT S. FOX, RONALD LIPPITT, and JOHN E. LOHMAN. *Teaching of Social Science Material in the Elementary School.* USOE Cooperative Research Project E-011. (ERIC ED 001 135) Ann Arbor, Michigan: University of Michigan.

110. JACK R. FRAENKEL. "A Curriculum Model for the Social Studies." *Social Education* 33: 41-47; January 1969.

111. DOROTHY M. FRASER, editor. "Review of Curriculum Materials." *Social Education* 33: 575-91; May 1969.

112. DOROTHY M. FRASER. "Status and Expectations of Current Research and Development Projects." *Social Education* 29: 421-34; November 1965.

113. DOROTHY McCLURE FRASER and SAMUEL P. McCUTCHEN, editors. *Social Studies in Transition: Guidelines for Change.* Washington, D.C.: National Council for the Social Studies, 1965. 67 pp.

114. VANCE CLARK FRASIER. "A Study of Students' Ability To Use Functional Imperatives as Strategies of Inquiry." Doctor's Dissertation, Columbia University, 1968. *Dissertation Abstracts* 29: 3911A; May 1969.

115. ALEXANDER FRAZIER. "Teacher Education Programs." In:

Alexander Frazier, editor. *Educating the Children of the Poor.* Washington, D.C.: Association for Supervision and Curriculum Development, 1968. pp. 16-21.

116. ALEXANDER FRAZIER. "The New Elementary School Teacher." In: Alexander Frazier, editor. *The New Elementary School.* Washington, D.C.: Association for Supervision and Curriculum Development, 1968. pp. 96-112.

117. ROBERT GAGNÉ. *The Conditions of Learning.* New York: Holt, Rinehart and Winston, Inc., 1965. 308 pp.

118. A. LAWRENCE GAGNON. "An Analysis of an Experimental Methodology for Teaching Thinking and Clarifying Values." Doctor's Dissertation, Wayne State University, 1965. *Dissertation Abstracts* 27: 1293A; November 1966.

119. MORRIS GALL. "Improving Competence in Judgment." *Social Education* 30: 88-90; February 1966.

120. MORRIS GALL. "The Current State of the Revolution in the Social Studies." *The Social Studies* 57: 242-45; November 1966.

121. WILLIAM E. GARDNER and ROMAN F. WARMKE. "Evaluating Programs in Economic Education." *Social Education* 30: 244-46; April 1966.

122. CHARLES R. GENGLER. "The Application of Geographical Terms to Map Symbolism." *Journal of Geography* 66: 394-96; October 1967.

123. JOHN GIBSON. *The Development of Instructional Materials Pertaining to Racial and Cultural Diversity in America.* USOE Project 5-1066. (ERIC ED 010 029) Medford, Massachusetts: Tufts University.

124. CLARK C. GILL. "How Eighth-Graders Interpret Indefinite Quantitative Concepts." *Social Education* 25: 344-46; November 1961.

125. CLARK C. GILL. "Interpretations of Indefinite Expressions of Time." *Social Education* 26: 454-56; December 1962.

126. CLARK GILL and WILLIAM CONROY. *Development of Guidelines and Resource Materials on Latin America for Use in Grades 1-12.* USOE Project 6-1183. (ERIC ED 012 365, ED 012 832, ED 013 542, ED 012 833, ED 012 632) Austin: University of Texas.

127. MARGARET CATHERINE GILLESPIE. "A Content Analysis of Selected Fifth Grade Basal Readers and Fifth Grade Social Studies Texts." Doctor's Dissertation, Stanford University, 1966. *Dissertation Abstracts* 27: 4164A; June 1967.

128. *Goals for Americans, The Report of the President's Commission on National Goals.* Englewood Cliffs, New Jersey: Prentice-Hall, Inc., 1960. 372 pp.

129. CHARLES MARION GODWIN. "Contemporary Practices in Selected Nebraska Elementary School Social Studies Programs." Doctor's Dissertation, The University of Nebraska Teachers College, 1967. *Dissertation Abstracts* 28: 3555A; March 1968.

130. GEORGE GOEBEL. "Reactions of Selected Sixth Grade Pupils to Social Studies Learning Activities Chosen by Their Teachers in the

Public Schools of Topeka, Kansas." Doctor's Dissertation, University of Kansas, 1965. *Dissertation Abstracts* 26: 3755-56; January 1966.

131. LORETTA GOLDEN. "The Treatment of Minority Groups in Primary Social Studies Textbooks." Doctor's Dissertation, Stanford University, 1964. *Dissertation Abstracts* 25: 3912; January 1965.

132. BERNICE GOLDMARK. "'Critical Thinking': Deliberate Method." *Social Education* 30: 329-34; May 1966.

133. PHINEAS GOLDSTEIN. "Concepts of Landforms and Waterforms of Children Beginning First Grade." Doctor's Dissertation, University of Southern California, 1966. *Dissertation Abstracts* 27: 1199A-1200A; November 1966.

134. JOHN I. GOODLAD, RENATA VON STOEPHASIUS, and M. FRANCES KLEIN. *The Changing School Curriculum.* New York: The Fund for the Advancement of Education, 1966. 122 pp.

135. THOMAS MORRIS GOOLSBY, JR. "Interrelationships Among Seven Measures of Competency in Elementary School Social Studies." Doctor's Dissertation, State University of Iowa, 1963. *Dissertation Abstracts* 24: 4540-41; May 1964.

136. RICHARD GORNICK. "A Study of the Relationship Between a Conceptual Framework and the Transference of Learning in the Social Studies." Doctor's Dissertation, Wayne State University, 1967. *Dissertation Abstracts* 29: 511A; August 1968.

137. JOSEPH CULVER GRANNIS. "An Experimental Study of the Inductive Learning of Abstract Social Concepts." Doctor's Dissertation, Washington University, 1965. *Dissertation Abstracts* 26: 4446; February 1966.

138. FREDERICK ELMAN GREEN. "Elementary School Children's Interests in the Social Studies as Revealed by a Forced Choice Questionnaire." Doctor's Dissertation, Ball State University, 1968. *Dissertation Abstracts* 29: 760A-61A; September 1968.

139. EDWARD LEONARD GREENBLATT. "An Exploratory Study of the Development of Selected Generalizations in Social Studies." Doctor's Dissertation, University of Southern California, 1963. *Dissertation Abstracts* 24: 3640-41; March 1964.

140. WILLIAM WASHINGTON GREENE, JR. "The Teaching of Anthropology in the First and Fourth Grades: A Comparison of Trained and Non-Trained Teachers as Measured by Pupil Test Performance." Doctor's Dissertation, University of Georgia, 1966. *Dissertation Abstracts* 27: 3339A-40A; April 1967.

141. FRED I. GREENSTEIN. *Children and Politics.* New Haven, Connecticut: Yale University Press, 1967. 199 pp.

142. RICHARD E. GROSS and RICHARD C. McCORMAC. "Video Tapes in the Preparation of the Social Studies Teacher." *Educational Screen and Audiovisual Guide* 46: 30-31; September 1967.

143. "Guidelines for the Preparation of Social Studies Teachers." *Social Education* 31: 490-91; October 1967.

144. CHARLES GUZETTA. "Children's Knowledge of Historically

Important Americans." Doctor's Dissertation, Temple University, 1964. *Dissertation Abstracts* 25: 1653-54; September 1964.

145. HARLAN HAHN. "Teacher Preparation in Political Science." *Social Education* 29: 86-89; February 1965.

146. DON E. HAMACHEK. *Motivation in Teaching and Learning.* What Research Says to the Teacher, No. 34. Washington, D.C.: Department of Classroom Teachers, National Education Association, 1968. 33 pp.

147. PAUL R. HANNA. "Design for a Social Studies Program." In: *Focus on the Social Studies.* Washington, D.C.: Department of Elementary School Principals, National Education Association, 1965. pp. 28-45.

148. PAUL R. HANNA and JOHN R. LEE. "Content in the Social Studies: Generalizations from the Social Sciences." In: John U. Michaelis, editor. *Social Studies in Elementary Schools.* Thirty-Second Yearbook. Washington, D.C.: National Council for the Social Studies, 1962. pp. 62-89.

149. JOHN HIRAM HANSEN. "The Social Studies Program of a Representative Sample of Wisconsin Junior High Schools and the Preparation of Social Studies Teachers." Doctor's Dissertation, The University of Wisconsin, 1964. *Dissertation Abstracts* 25: 2365-66; October 1964.

150. DONALD WILLIAM HARDY. "Inland Valley Elementary School Archaeology Project: An Experimental Comparison of Two Teaching Approaches." Doctor's Dissertation, University of California at Berkeley, 1967. *Dissertation Abstracts* 29: 61A-62A; July 1968.

151. BERJ HAROOTUNIAN and MERLE W. TATE. "The Relationship of Certain Selected Variables to Problem Solving Ability." *The Journal of Educational Psychology* 51: 326-33; December 1960.

152. ROBERT HARNACK. *The Use of Electronic Computers To Improve Individualization of Instruction Through Unit Teaching.* USOE 5-0723. (ERIC ED 003 391) Buffalo: State University of New York.

153. IRENE E. HARNEY and LUCILLE P. BURGDORF. "Urban Children Study Interaction Among People." *The Instructor* 78: 92-94; December 1968.

154. JUDAH J. HARRIS. "The Treatment of Religion in Elementary School Social Studies Textbooks." In: Wayne L. Herman, Jr., editor. *Current Research in Elementary School Social Studies.* New York: The Macmillan Company, 1969. pp. 400-404.

155. LILLIAN HARMON HEIL. "Wonder Tales in Social Studies Programs of the Primary Grades." Doctor's Dissertation, Columbia University, 1968. *Dissertation Abstracts* 29: 4376A-77A; June 1969.

156. ROSA MAY HENSON. "A Measurement of Social Studies Achievement in the Primary Grades." Doctor's Dissertation, North Texas State University, 1963. *Dissertation Abstracts* 25: 934-35; August 1964.

157. SISTER JOSEPH HENZL. *Adapting the Spiral Curriculum and Discovery Learning to the Teaching of Geography.* USOE Project 7-1025. Seattle: Holy Name Academy.

158. WAYNE L. HERMAN, JR. "An Analysis of the Activities and Verbal Behavior in Selected Fifth-Grade Social Studies Classes." *The Journal of Educational Research* 60: 339-45; April 1967.

159. WAYNE L. HERMAN, JR., editor. *Current Research in Elementary School Social Studies.* New York: The Macmillan Company, 1969. 468 pp.

160. WAYNE L. HERMAN, JR. "How Intermediate Children Rank the Subjects." *The Journal of Educational Research* 56: 435-36; April 1963.

161. WAYNE L. HERMAN, JR. "The Relationship Between Teachers' Verbal Behavior and Children's Interests in the Social Studies." *Peabody Journal of Education* 43: 157-60; November 1965.

162. WAYNE L. HERMAN, JR. "The Use of Language Arts in Social Studies Lessons." *American Educational Research Journal* 4: 117-24; March 1967.

163. ROBERT HESS and DAVID EASTON. *The Development of Basic Attitudes and Values Toward Government and Citizenship During the Elementary School Years.* USOE Cooperative Research Project 1078-FT-1. (ERIC ED 010 119) Chicago: University of Chicago.

164. ROBERT D. HESS and DAVID EASTON. "The Role of the Elementary School in Political Socialization." *The School Review* 70: 257-65; Autumn 1962.

165. ROBERT D. HESS and JUDITH B. TORNEY. *The Development of Political Attitudes in Children.* Chicago: Aldine Publishing Company, 1967. 288 pp.

166. LOIS ANN HIGH. "A Critical Analysis of Political Concepts in Sixth Grade Geography Textbooks." Doctor's Dissertation, Baylor University, 1968. *Dissertation Abstracts* 29: 1363A; November 1968.

167. WILHELMINA HILL. *Social Studies in the Elementary School Program.* Washington, D.C.: U.S. Department of Health, Education, and Welfare, 1960. 110 pp.

168. JAMES LAFAYETTE HILLS. "Dimensions of Children's Learning About Social Studies Generalizations." Doctor's Dissertation, University of Southern California, 1964. *Dissertation Abstracts* 25: 3431-32; December 1964.

169. JOHN HOLT. *How Children Learn.* New York: Pitman Publishing Corporation, 1967. 189 pp.

170. FRANCIS P. HUNKINS. "The Influence of Analysis and Evaluation Questions on Achievement in Sixth Grade Social Studies." *Educational Leadership* 25: 326-32; January 1968.

171. FRANCIS PETER HUNKINS. "The Influence of Analysis and Evaluation Questions on Critical Thinking and Achievement in Sixth Grade Social Studies." Doctor's Dissertation, Kent State University, 1966. *Dissertation Abstracts* 28: 538A; August 1967. (Also *Educational Leadership Research Supplement* 1: 326-32; January 1968.)

172. FRANCIS P. HUNKINS and PHYLLIS SHAPIRO. "Teaching

Critical Thinking in Elementary Social Studies." *Education* 88: 68-72; September-October 1967.

173. DONALD AMMUNN INGLI. "An Audio-Visual Approach to the Intermediate Grade Social Studies." Doctor's Dissertation, University of Wisconsin, 1961. *Dissertation Abstracts* 21: 2967; April 1961.

174. LEONARD W. INGRAHAM. "The 'Mixed Media' Menu." *Social Education* 31: 698-700; December 1967.

175. AGNES M. S. INN. "Beginning Teachers' Problems in Developing Social Studies Concepts." *Social Education* 30: 540-41; November 1966.

176. *INSITE: Instructional Systems in Teacher Education.* Fourth Annual Report to the Ford Foundation, Part III. Bloomington, Indiana: Indiana University, 1967. 74 pp.

177. MARGARET JEAN IRVIN. "A Survey of Educational Preparation and Basic Problems of Social Studies Teachers in Selected Junior High Schools of the North Central Association Region, with Recommendations for Teacher Preparation." Doctor's Dissertation, Arizona State University, 1967. *Dissertation Abstracts* 27: 2916A-17A; March 1967.

178. JOHN JAROLIMEK. *Guidelines for Elementary Social Studies.* Washington, D.C.: Association for Supervision and Curriculum Development, 1967. 33 pp.

179. JOHN JAROLIMEK and CLIFFORD D. FOSTER. "Quantitative Concepts in Fifth-Grade Social-Studies Textbooks." *The Elementary School Journal* 59: 437-42; May 1959.

180. JOHN JAROLIMEK and others. "The Tri-University Project in Elementary Education" and other articles. *The College of Education Record* 34: 59-101; May 1968.

181. DEAN JAROS. "Children's Orientations Toward the President: Some Additional Considerations and Data." *The Journal of Politics* 29: 368-87; May 1967.

182. DEAN JAROS, HERBERT HIRSCH, and FREDERIC J. FLERON, JR. "The Malevolent Leader: Political Socialization in an American Sub-Culture." *The American Political Science Review* 62: 564-75; June 1968.

183. WILLIAM JOHN JEFFERDS. "A Comparison of Two Methods of Teaching Economics in Grade One." Doctor's Dissertation, University of California at Berkeley, 1966. *Dissertation Abstracts* 27: 3620A; May 1967.

184. JAMES E. JESTER, JR. "A Comparative Study of the Effects of Team Teaching and Departmentalized Teaching on the Scholastic Achievement of Eighth Grade Students in Social Studies and Language Arts." Doctor's Dissertation, University of Kansas, 1966. *Dissertation Abstracts* 28: 1002A-1003A; September 1967.

185. A. ELIZABETH JOHNSON. "Discovering Generalizations Regarding Africa South of the Sahara Held by Certain Sixth Grade Students and by Certain University Seniors, and Determining the Signifi-

cance of These Generalizations for the Content of the Social Studies Curriculum." Doctor's Dissertation, Wayne State University, 1966. *Dissertation Abstracts* 27: 2280A-81A; February 1967.

186. CARL JOHNSON and CHARLES DAMBACH. *Survey of Printed Materials on Conservation Education.* USOE Project 5-1058. (ERIC ED 014 434) Columbus, Ohio: Ohio State University Research Foundation.

187. RALPH MORRIS JOHNSON. "A Critical Analysis of the Treatments Given Representative Social Science Ideas in Leading Fifth and Eighth Grade American History Textbooks." Doctor's Dissertation, Northwestern University, 1967. *Dissertation Abstracts* 28: 1988A; December 1967.

188. ANDREW VANCE JOHNSTON. "An Investigation of Elementary School Teachers' Information, Concepts and Generalizations About Races, Cultures and Nations." Doctor's Dissertation, University of Georgia, 1963. *Dissertation Abstracts* 25: 1654; September 1964.

189. ARTHUR HERBERT JONAS. "A Study of the Relationship of Certain Behaviors of Children to Emotional Needs, Values, and Thinking." Doctor's Dissertation, New York University, 1960. *Dissertation Abstracts* 21: 3018-19; April 1961.

190. RITA HONKAVAARA JONES. "Relationships Between Two Modes of Social Studies Instruction." Doctor's Dissertation, University of California at Berkeley, 1964. *Dissertation Abstracts* 25: 4001-4002; January 1965.

191. BRUCE JOYCE. "Social Sciencing—New Concept in Social Studies." *The Instructor* 78: 85-92; October 1968.

192. BRUCE JOYCE. *Use of Data Storage and Retrieval System To Teach Elementary School Children Concepts and Modes of Inquiry in the Social Sciences.* USOE Project 5-1369. (ERIC ED 018 671) New York: Teachers College, Columbia University.

193. BRUCE JOYCE and ELIZABETH JOYCE. "Searching for Strategies for Social Education." *The Elementary School Journal* 66: 272-83; February 1966.

194. BRUCE JOYCE and CARL WEINBERG. "Using the Strategies of Sociology in Social Education." *The Elementary School Journal* 64: 265-72; February 1964.

195. WILLIAM WALTER JOYCE. "The Development and Grade Placement of Map and Globe Skills in the Elementary Social Studies Program." Doctor's Dissertation, Northwestern University, 1964. *Dissertation Abstracts* 25: 6434-35; May 1965.

196. THEODORE KALTSOUNIS. "A Study Concerning Third Graders' Knowledge of Social Studies Content Prior to Instruction." Doctor's Dissertation, University of Illinois, 1961. *Dissertation Abstracts* 22: 1528-29; November 1961.

197. THEODORE KALTSOUNIS. "Current Basic Principles in Social Sciences." *Education* 84: 274-79; January 1964.

198. THEODORE KALTSOUNIS. "The Gap That Must Be Bridged." *Social Education* 32: 699-703; November 1968.

199. EDWARD ANOEL KARNS. "Teacher and Pupil Attitudes Toward Textbooks and Instructional Television as Authoritative Sources of Information in Sixth Grade Social Studies." Doctor's Dissertation, Kent State University, 1966. *Dissertation Abstracts* 28: 393A-94A; August 1967.

200. JOHN WILLIAM KELLY. "An Analysis and Evaluation of a Coordinated Master-Teacher Program in Social Studies and in Science at the Fifth-Grade Level." Doctor's Dissertation, Fordham University, 1967. *Dissertation Abstracts* 28: 3560A-61A; March 1968.

201. BERNARD GRIFFIN KIRSCH. "An Evaluation of Levels of Cognitive Learning in a Unit of Fifth Grade Social Studies." Doctor's Dissertation, University of Southern California, 1967. *Dissertation Abstracts* 28: 541A; August 1967.

202. ALBERT KLEVAN. "An Investigation of a Methodology for Value Clarification: Its Relationship to Consistency in Thinking, Purposefulness, and Human Relations." Doctor's Dissertation, New York University, 1957. *Dissertation Abstracts* 18: 1732; May 1958.

203. ROBERT DONALD KRANYIK. "A Comparison of the Images of Mexico Portrayed in Elementary Social Studies Textbooks and Possessed by Connecticut and Mexican Teachers." Doctor's Dissertation, The University of Connecticut, 1965. *Dissertation Abstracts* 26: 5295; March 1966.

204. DAVID R. KRATHWOHL, BENJAMIN S. BLOOM, and BERTRAM B. MASIA. *Taxonomy of Educational Objectives: Handbook II, Affective Domain.* New York: David McKay Company, Inc., 1964. 196 pp.

205. MARK M. KRUG. "Bruner's New Social Studies: A Critique." *Social Education* 30: 400-406; October 1966.

206. DANA KURFMAN. "A National Assessment of Social Studies Education." *Social Education* 31: 209-11; March 1967.

207. WALLACE E. LAMBERT and OTTO KLINEBERG. *Children's Views of Foreign Peoples.* New York: Appleton-Century-Crofts, Inc., 1967. 319 pp.

208. AMASA GUY LARKINS. "Assessing Achievement on a First-Grade Economics Course of Study." Doctor's Dissertation, Utah State University, 1968. *Dissertation Abstracts* 29: 1366A-67A; November 1968.

209. GENE LAWRENCE LAVENDER. "The Prediction of Social Studies Teachers' Success Through the Use of Credentials." Doctor's Dissertation, The University of Nebraska Teachers College, 1968. *Dissertation Abstracts* 29: 1717A-18A; December 1968.

210. HOPE MARILYN HALENBECK LEA. "A Study of Some Characteristics of the Variability of Teacher Activities in the Social Studies and Pupil Response and Achievement." Doctor's Dissertation, University of Minnesota, 1964. *Dissertation Abstracts* 26: 2590; November 1965.

211. JOHN R. LEE. "Northwestern University, Materials for a New Approach to American History." *Social Education* 29: 223; April 1965.

212. JOHN R. LEE. *Social Studies Curriculum Center: A Sequen-*

108   ELEMENTARY SCHOOL SOCIAL STUDIES

tial Curriculum on American Society for Grades 5-12. USOE Project 5-0675. Evanston, Illinois: Northwestern University.

213. JOHN R. LEE and NATHANIEL STAMPFER. "Two Studies in Learning Geography: Implications for the Primary Grades." *Social Education* 30: 627-28; December 1966.

214. LULA MYRTLE LEEF. "The Evolution of Twentieth Century Elementary Social Studies Instruction in Relation to Social, Political, and Economic Conditions." Doctor's Dissertation, University of Idaho, 1966. *Dissertation Abstracts* 28: 947A; September 1967.

215. C. L. JOHN LEGERE. "An Investigation of Time Relationship Understandings in Grades Four Through Eight." Doctor's Dissertation, Boston University School of Education, 1962. *Dissertation Abstracts* 23: 1625; November 1962.

216. LEWIS EARL LEMMOND. "A Value Analysis of Social Studies Textbooks." Doctor's Dissertation, East Texas State College, 1964. *Dissertation Abstracts* 26: 798; August 1965.

217. RONALD LIPPITT, PEGGY LIPPITT, and ROBERT FOX. "A Laboratory Approach to Social Science Education." *International Review of Education* 11: 351-58; 1965.

218. RONALD LIPPITT, PEGGY LIPPITT, and ROBERT FOX. "Children Look at Their Own Behavior." *Today's Education* (formerly *NEA Journal*) 53: 14-16; September 1964.

219. WILFRED W. LISKE. "An Investigation of the Readability of Selected Juvenile Encyclopedia Material by the Cloze Procedure and a Comparison of Results with Readability Formulas." In: Wayne L. Herman, Jr., editor. *Current Research in Elementary School Social Studies.* New York: The Macmillan Company, 1969. pp. 363-68.

220. HAROLD M. LONG and ROBERT N. KING. *Improving the Teaching of World Affairs: The Glens Falls Story.* Washington, D.C.: National Council for the Social Studies, 1964. 92 pp.

221. BETTY LUCILLE LOWRY. "A Survey of the Knowledge of Social Studies Concepts Possessed by Second Grade Children Previous to the Time These Concepts Are Taught in the Social Studies Lessons." Doctor's Dissertation, State University of Iowa, 1963. *Dissertation Abstracts* 24: 2324-25; December 1963.

222. JOHN E. LUX. "A Comparison of Teaching Methods Used by Superior and Non-Superior Teachers." *The Social Studies* 53: 171-74; October 1962.

223. W. J. LYDA and VERNA A. ROBINSON. "Quantitative Concepts in Selected Social Studies Textbooks for Second Grade." *The Elementary School Journal* 65: 159-62; December 1964.

224. G. A. MADDOX and R. S. ROSS. "Strong Words." *Childhood Education* 45: 260-64; January 1969.

225. MARTIN MAYER. *The Schools.* New York: Harper and Bros., 1961. 446 pp.

226. J. D. McAULAY. "Controversial Issues in the Social Studies." *Education* 86: 27-30; September 1965.

227. J. D. McAulay. "Some Map Abilities of Second Grade Children." *Journal of Geography* 61: 3-9; January 1962.

228. J. D. McAulay. "Weaknesses in the Social Studies Methods Courses." *Education* 81: 245-46; December 1960.

229. J. D. McAulay. "What Understandings Do Second Grade Children Have of Time Relationships?" *Journal of Educational Research* 54: 312-14; April 1961.

230. Anthony H. McNaughton and others. "The Use of Teaching Modules To Study High-Level Thinking in the Social Studies." *The Journal of Teacher Education* 18: 495-502; Winter 1967.

231. James Merritt. "A Study of Sixth Graders' Comprehension of Specially-Prepared Materials on Broad Social Conflicts." *The Journal of Educational Research* 61: 328-33; March 1968.

232. Lawrence E. Metcalf. "Some Guidelines for Changing Social Studies Education." *Social Education* 27: 197-201; April 1963.

233. Alice Miel. "New Patterns of In-Service Education of Elementary Teachers." In: Alexander Frazier, editor. *The New Elementary School.* Washington, D.C.: Association for Supervision and Curriculum Development, 1968. pp. 68-95.

234. Alice Miel and Edwin Kiester, Jr. *The Shortchanged Children of Suburbia.* New York: Institute of Human Relations Press, 1967. 68 pp.

235. Jack W. Miller. "Measuring Perspective Ability." *Journal of Geography* 66: 167-71; April 1967.

236. Martha Browder Monroe. "A Study of Changes in Specifically Identified Social Behaviors in a Fifth Grade Class by Means of an Individualized Social Studies Program." Doctor's Dissertation, University of Utah, 1969. *Dissertation Abstracts* 30: 215A; July 1969.

237. Jay Albert Monson. "An Analysis of Programs of Utah Universities and Colleges Preparing Elementary School Teachers for Teaching Social Studies." Doctor's Dissertation, Utah State University, 1968. *Dissertation Abstracts* 29: 2136A-37A; January 1969.

238. Irving Morrissett, editor. *Concepts and Structure in the New Social Science Curricula.* New York: Holt, Rinehart and Winston, Inc., 1967. 161 pp.

239. Irving Morrissett. *Social Science Education Consortium: Research and Development for Grades K-12.* USOE Project 5-0619. (ERIC ED 013 994—ED 014 006; ED 010 085—010 086) Lafayette, Indiana: Purdue University.

240. Irving Morrissett and W. Williams Stevens, Jr. "Curriculum Analysis." *Social Education* 31: 483-86, 489; October 1967.

241. Mignonette Harrison Mountain. "Educational Games for Classroom Use." Doctor's Dissertation, The Pennsylvania State University, 1960. *Dissertation Abstracts* 21: 1873; January 1961.

242. Dorothy J. Mugge. "Are Young Children Ready To Study the Social Sciences?" *The Elementary School Journal* 68: 232-40; February 1968.

243. DOROTHY J. MUGGE. "Precocity of Today's Young Children: Real or Wishful?" *Social Education* 27: 436-39; December 1963.

244. National Council for the Social Studies. "The Role of the Social Studies." *Social Education* 26: 315-18, 327; October 1962.

245. FRED M. NEWMANN. "Evaluation of Programed Instruction in the Social Studies." *Social Education* 29: 291-95; May 1965.

246. HOMER RICHWELL PANKEY. "A Study of the Economic Education Workshops in Developing Teacher Awareness of Economic Understandings." Doctor's Dissertation, West Virginia University, 1967. *Dissertation Abstracts* 28: 2910A; February 1968.

247. DAVID MICHAEL PENDERGAST. "A Study of Changes in Role Perceptions Held by Beginning Social Studies Teachers." Doctor's Dissertation, The Ohio State University, 1967. *Dissertation Abstracts* 28: 3534A; March 1968.

248. ORVILLE KENNETH PENNER. "A Study of Fourth Grade Children's Knowledge of Selected Social Studies Concepts Prior to Instruction." Doctor's Dissertation, Colorado State College, 1967. *Dissertation Abstracts* 28: 403A; August 1967.

249. ALEX F. PERRODIN. "Factors Affecting the Development of Cooperation in Children." *The Journal of Educational Research* 53: 283-88; April 1960.

250. VITO PERRONE. *Image of Latin America: A Study of American School Textbooks and School Children, Grades 2-12.* USOE Project 5-8105. (ERIC ED 003 454) Marquette, Michigan: Northern Michigan University.

251. EDWARD G. PONDER. "Some Psycho-Social Phenomena of the Disadvantaged and Social Studies Learning." *Social Education* 33: 61-65; January 1969.

252. DRORA PORTUGALY. "A Study of the Development of Disadvantaged Kindergarten Children's Understanding of the Earth as a Globe." Doctor's Dissertation, Columbia University, 1967. *Dissertation Abstracts* 28: 4056A; April 1968.

253. WILMA MARTENS POSSIEN. "A Comparison of the Effects of Three Methodologies on the Development of the Problem-Solving Skills of Sixth Grade Children." Doctor's Dissertation, University of Alabama, 1964. *Dissertation Abstracts* 25: 4003; January 1965.

254. JAMES EDWARD POTTERFIELD. "An Analysis of Elementary School Children's Ability To Learn Anthropological Content at Grades Four, Five, and Six." Doctor's Dissertation, University of Georgia, 1966. *Dissertation Abstracts* 27: 1721A; December 1966. (Also in *Journal of Educational Research* 61: 297-99; March 1968.)

255. ROY A. PRICE, editor. *Needed Research in the Teaching of the Social Studies.* Washington, D.C.: National Council for the Social Studies, 1964. 126 pp.

256. ROY A. PRICE. "Syracuse University, School Science Concepts and Workways as the Basis for Curriculum Revision." *Social Education* 29: 218-20; April 1965.

257. ROY A. PRICE, GERALD R. SMITH, and WARREN L. HICKMAN. *Major Concepts for the Social Studies.* Syracuse, New York: Social Studies Curriculum Center, Syracuse University, 1965. 68 pp.

258. *Professional Growth Requirements, 1965-66.* Washington, D.C.: National Education Association Research Division, 1966. 32 pp.

259. WILLIAM D. RADER. *Materials for Elementary School Economics Program (Grades 4 and 5).* Chicago: Industrial Relations Center, University of Chicago.

260. WILLIAM B. RAGAN and JOHN D. MCAULAY. *Social Studies for Today's Children.* New York: Appleton-Century-Crofts, Inc., 1964. 409 pp.

261. EVALYN BARBARA ROGERS RAPPARLIE. "Descriptive Analysis of a Problem-Solving Approach to the Teaching of Critical Thinking with Primary Children." Doctor's Dissertation, University of Illinois, 1968. *Dissertation Abstracts* 30: 221A; July 1969.

262. JAMES RATHS. "Clarifying Children's Values." *The National Elementary Principal* 42: 35-39; November 1962.

263. JAMES RATHS. "Underachievement and a Search for Values." *Sociology of Education* 34: 422-24; May 1961.

264. *Report of the State Central Committee on Social Studies to the California State Curriculum Commission.* Sacramento, California: California State Department of Education, 1961. 92 pp.

265. MARION J. RICE. "Improving Elementary Geography." *The Elementary School Journal* 66: 126-38; December 1965.

266. MARION J. RICE and WILFRED C. BAILEY. "University of Georgia, A Sequential Curriculum in Anthropology for Grades 1-7." *Social Education* 29: 211-12; April 1965.

267. LEONOR MAY RICH. "The Effectiveness of Individual and Team Assignments Following Mass Presentations in Social Studies in Grades Four, Five, and Six." Doctor's Dissertation, Boston University School of Education, 1968. *Dissertation Abstracts* 29: 4389A-90A; June 1969.

268. H. ALAN ROBINSON. "Reading Skills Employed in Solving Social Studies Problems." *The Reading Teacher* 18: 263-69; January 1965.

269. VINCENT R. ROGERS. "Developing Sensitivity and Concern in Children." *Social Education* 31: 299-302; April 1967.

270. VINCENT R. ROGERS and DOROTHY E. LAYTON. "An Exploratory Study of Primary Grade Children's Ability To Conceptualize Based Upon Content Drawn from Selected Social Studies Topics." *The Journal of Educational Research* 59: 195-97; January 1966.

271. VINCENT R. ROGERS and ELIZABETH LONG. "An Exploratory Study of the Development of Social Sensitivity in Elementary School Children." *The Journal of Educational Research* 59: 392-94; May-June 1966.

272. DANIEL ROSELLE. "Citizenship Goals for a New Age." *Social Education* 30: 415-20; October 1966.

112   ELEMENTARY SCHOOL SOCIAL STUDIES

273. D. LILYAN RUDERMAN. "An Exploration of Empathic Ability in Children and Its Relationship to Several Variables." Doctor's Dissertation, Columbia University, 1961. *Dissertation Abstracts* 23: 1414-15; October 1962.

274. HAIG A. RUSHDOONY. "Achievement in Map-Reading; An Experimental Study." *The Elementary School Journal* 64: 70-75; November 1963.

275. MARY RUSNACK. "Introducing Social Studies in the First Grade." *Social Education* 25: 291-92; October 1961.

276. FRANK L. RYAN. "Four Methods of Using Programed Materials in Social Studies." Doctor's Dissertation, University of California at Berkeley, 1966. *Dissertation Abstracts* 27: 2453A; February 1967.

277. FRANK L. RYAN. "Teacher Inclusion in a Programmed Instructional Sequence Involving Social Studies Content." *The Journal of Educational Research* 62: 53-57; October 1968.

278. HELEN SAGL. "Problem Solving, Inquiry, Discovery?" *Childhood Education* 43: 137-41; November 1966.

279. NORRIS M. SANDERS. *Classroom Questions.* New York: Harper & Row, Publishers, 1966. 176 pp.

280. PHILLIP SAUNDERS. "Preparing Future Teachers for Economic Competence: Content Appraisal." *Social Education* 30: 247-50; April 1966.

281. JOHN F. SAVAGE. "Elaborative Thinking—Done Better in Groups." *The Elementary School Journal* 64: 434-37; May 1964.

282. PAUL E. SCHIELE. "An Analysis of Children's Concepts of Common Sixth Grade Social Studies Terms." Master's Thesis, Claremont Graduate School, 1961. 102 pp.

283. SISTER MARY PHILOMENE SCHILLER. "The Effects of the Functional Use of Certain Skills in Seventh-Grade Social Studies." *The Journal of Educational Research* 57: 201-203; December 1963.

284. DONALD LEE SCHILSON. "Problems of Beginning Teachers in Teaching Elementary Social Studies." Doctor's Dissertation, State University of Iowa, 1962. *Dissertation Abstracts* 23: 1561; November 1962.

285. CLARENCE WILLIAM SCHMINKE. "A Study of the Effective Utilization of a Classroom News Magazine in Teaching Current Events." Doctor's Dissertation, State University of Iowa, 1960. *Dissertation Abstracts* 21: 1874-75; January 1961.

286. VIRGINIA SCHNEPF. "A Study of Political Socialization in a Subculture: Negro Children's Knowledge of and Attitudes Toward the Police, Law and Freedom." Doctor's Dissertation, University of Illinois, 1966. *Dissertation Abstracts* 27: 2016A; January 1967.

287. CARL EDWARD SCHOMBURG. "A Study of the Presentation and Reenforcement of Geographic Concepts Found in Selected Geography Textbooks in Adoption in the State of Texas During 1964-65." Doctor's Dissertation, University of Houston, 1966. *Dissertation Abstracts* 27: 2752A; March 1967.

288. JOAN EMELIA SCHREIBER. "Teachers' Question-Asking Techniques in Social Studies." Doctor's Dissertation, The University of Iowa, 1967. *Dissertation Abstracts* 28: 523A; August 1967.

289. HERBERT SCHUELER, MILTON J. GOLD, and HAROLD P. MITZEL. *The Use of Television for Improving Teacher Training and for Improving Measures of Student-Teaching Performance, Phase I. Improvement of Student Teaching.* Project NDEA-VII-068-1. (ERIC ED 003 510) New York: Hunter College, City University of New York.

290. VERNON ANDREW SCHUMACHER. "Fifth and Sixth Grade Students' Understanding of Surface Features of the Earth." Doctor's Dissertation, State University of Iowa, 1961. *Dissertation Abstracts* 22: 2638; February 1962.

291. MICHAEL SCRIVEN. "Values in the Curriculum." *Social Science Education Consortium Newsletter* 2: 1-3; 1966.

292. LAWRENCE SENESH. *Elkhart Indiana Experiment in Economic Education.* Lafayette, Indiana: Purdue University Department of Economics.

293. LAWRENCE SENESH. *"Our Working World" Series.* Chicago: Science Research Associates, 1967.

294. LAWRENCE SENESH. "The Pattern of the Economic Curriculum." *Social Education* 32: 47-50, 59; January 1968.

295. *Sequential Tests of Educational Progress: Social Studies, Form 4.* Princeton, New Jersey: Cooperative Test Division, Educational Testing Service, 1957.

296. RICHARD E. SERVEY. *Social Studies Instruction in the Elementary School.* San Francisco: Chandler Publishing Company, 1967. 565 pp.

297. GEORGE SHAFTEL and FANNIE SHAFTEL. *Role-Playing for Social Values.* Englewood Cliffs, New Jersey: Prentice-Hall, Inc., 1967. 431 pp.

298. JACK MICHAEL SHERIDAN. "An Investigation of Beginning First Grade Children's Awareness Regarding a Selected Number of Concepts of Physical Geography." Doctor's Dissertation, University of Oregon, 1964. *Dissertation Abstracts* 25: 5649-50; April 1965.

299. JACK M. SHERIDAN. "Children's Awareness of Physical Geography." *Journal of Geography* 67: 82-86; February 1968.

300. RIDGWAY F. SHINN, JR. *An Investigation into the Utilization of Geography and History as Integrating Disciplines for Social Studies Curricular Development in a Public School System.* USOE Project E-028. (ERIC ED 003 393) Providence, Rhode Island: Rhode Island College.

301. THOMAS ALONZO SINKS. "How Individualized Instruction in Junior High School Science, Mathematics, Language Arts, and Social Studies Affects Student Achievement." Doctor's Dissertation, University of Illinois, 1968. *Dissertation Abstracts* 30: 224A-25A; July 1969.

302. LYLE LENARD SKOV. "The Teaching-Learning of Factual Information in the Social Sciences in a Program That Is Deliberately

Structured To Promote Social Learnings for Democratic Behavior." Doctor's Dissertation, University of Arkansas, 1962. *Dissertation Abstracts* 22: 4283-84; June 1962.

303. ARNOLD ALTON SLAN. "A Comparison of Two Techniques for the Teaching of Current Affairs at the Intermediate Grades." Doctor's Dissertation, Indiana University, 1966. *Dissertation Abstracts* 27: 1722A-23A; December 1966.

304. FRANK SMITH. "Methods Courses as Seen by Students." *Improving College and University Teaching* 14: 120-21; Spring 1966.

305. GERALD R. SMITH. "Project Social Studies—A Report." *Social Education* 27: 357-59, 409; November 1963.

306. LLOYD L. SMITH. "Current Events for the Elementary School." *Social Education* 25: 75-78, 81; February 1961.

307. RONALD O. SMITH and CHARLES F. CARDINELL. "Challenging the Expanding-Environment Theory." *Social Education* 28: 141-43; March 1964.

308. TWILA MILLER WAKEFIELD SMITH. "The Place of History in Elementary School Social Studies: A Proposed Program To Include the Role of Negro Americans." Doctor's Dissertation, The University of Texas, 1967. *Dissertation Abstracts* 28: 1736A; November 1967.

309. Proposed *Social Sciences Education Framework for California Public Schools: Report of the Statewide Social Sciences Study Committee to the State Curriculum Commission and the California State Board of Education.* Sacramento, California: California State Board of Education, 1968. 186 pp.

310. SOL SPEARS. "Children's Concept Learning in Economics Under Three Experimental Curricula." Doctor's Dissertation, University of California at Los Angeles, 1967. *Dissertation Abstracts* 28: 2462A; January 1968.

311. BERNARD SPODEK. "Developing Social Studies Concepts in the Kindergarten." *Social Education* 27: 253-56; May 1963.

312. NATHANIEL STAMPFER. "A Study of Map Skills Attainment in Selected Middle Grades." Doctor's Dissertation, Northwestern University, 1966. *Dissertation Abstracts* 27: 2102A; January 1967.

313. LOIS EVANS STEPHENS. "What Concepts of Telling Time Can Be Developed by Kindergarten Children." Doctor's Dissertation, University of California at Los Angeles, 1964. *Dissertation Abstracts* 25: 1793-94; September 1964.

314. JAMES HOWARD STITT. "Effects of Instruction on Children's Inferential Thinking." Doctor's Dissertation, University of California at Los Angeles, 1967. *Dissertation Abstracts* 28: 3083A-84A; February 1968.

315. SONJA H. STONE. "Chicago's Center for Inner City Studies: An Experiment in Relevancy." *Social Education* 33: 528-32; May 1969.

316. FLORENCE STRATEMEYER and others. *Developing a Curriculum for Modern Living.* New York: Bureau of Publications, Teachers College, Columbia University, 1957. 740 pp.

317. J. RICHARD SUCHMAN. "Inquiry in the Curriculum." *Instructor* 75: 24, 64; January 1966.

318. HILDA TABA. *Development of a Comprehensive Curriculum Model for Social Studies, Grades 1-8, Including Procedures for Implementation.* San Francisco: San Francisco State College.

319. HILDA TABA. *Teacher's Handbook for Elementary Social Studies.* Palo Alto, California: Addison-Wesley Publishing Company, 1967. 150 pp.

320. HILDA TABA. *Teaching Strategies and Cognitive Functioning in Elementary School Children.* USOE Project 2404. San Francisco: San Francisco State College.

321. HILDA TABA. "Teaching Strategy and Learning." *California Journal for Instructional Improvement* 6: 3-11; December 1963.

322. HILDA TABA. "Techniques of In-Service Training." *Social Education* 29: 464-76; November 1965.

323. HILDA TABA, SAMUEL LEVINE, and FREEMAN F. ELZEY. *Thinking in Elementary School Children.* USOE Cooperative Research Project 1574. (ERIC ED 003 285) San Francisco: San Francisco State College, 1964.

324. *The Taba Social Studies Curriculum.* Menlo Park, California: Addison-Wesley Publishing Company, 1969.

325. RONALD HARRY TALI. "The Use of Programed Materials for Teaching in the Social Studies." Doctor's Dissertation, The University of Michigan, 1967. *Dissertation Abstracts* 28: 2001A; December 1967.

326. GEORGELLE THOMAS. "Programmed Instruction for Teaching Anthropology in the Fifth Grade." *The Journal of Experimental Education* 36: 88-92; Summer 1968.

327. WILLIAM ADAM THOMPSON. "The Development of Supplementary Economic Curriculum Content Materials and Evaluation of Their Use with Fifth Grade Students." Doctor's Dissertation, University of Missouri, 1966. *Dissertation Abstracts* 27: 2958A; March 1967.

328. JOHN O. TOWLER and L. D. NELSON. "The Elementary School Child's Concept of Scale." *Journal of Geography* 67: 24-28; January 1968.

329. CLARK DUANE TUFTE. "The Use of Higher Level Questions for Diagnosis of Existing and Evaluation of Developing Attitudes in Elementary Social Studies." Doctor's Dissertation, The University of North Dakota, 1968. *Dissertation Abstracts* 29: 3926A-27A; May 1969.

330. RICHARD L. TURNER and NICHOLAS A. FATTU. *Skill in Teaching, A Reappraisal of the Concepts and Strategies in Teacher Effectiveness Research.* Bloomington, Indiana: Indiana University School of Education, May 1960. 40 pp.

331. GLENYS G. UNRUH. "Urban Relevance and the Social Studies Curriculum." *Social Education* 33: 708-11; October 1969.

332. DAVID THEODORE USLAN. "A Study of Geographic and Related Physical Science Concepts and Understandings Attainable Through

the Media of School Radio Communication." Doctor's Dissertation, University of California at Los Angeles, 1964. *Dissertation Abstracts* 25: 5800-5801; April 1965.

333. JAMES J. VELTKAMP. "An Analysis of the Status of Geography Education in the Intermediate Grades in a Tri-State Regional Area." Doctor's Dissertation, University of South Dakota, 1967. *Dissertation Abstracts* 28: 1635A-36A; November 1967.

334. DONALD FIELD VORREYER. "An Analysis of Teacher Classroom Behavior and Role." Doctor's Dissertation, University of Maryland, 1965. *Dissertation Abstracts* 26: 5254; March 1966.

335. RICHARD WALLACE. *The Ability of Certain Pupils To Understand and Apply Selected Concepts and Generalizations in Geography.* USOE Project 5-8426. (ERIC ED 010 091) Chestnut Hill, Massachusetts: Boston College.

336. KENNETH D. WANN, MIRIAM SELCHEN DORN, and ELIZABETH ANN LIDDLE. *Fostering Intellectual Development in Young Children.* New York: Bureau of Publications, Teachers College, Columbia University, 1962. 140 pp.

337. ANN ROREM WATTS. "Conceptual Clarification of Certain Geographic Terms Through the Use of Five Presentation Modes." Doctor's Dissertation, The University of Oklahoma, 1965. *Dissertation Abstracts* 26: 1519; September 1965.

338. CARROLL EUGENE WEBER. "A Study of Sixth-Grade Children's Ability To Infer the Influence of the Natural Environment Upon Man." Doctor's Dissertation, University of California at Berkeley, 1964. *Dissertation Abstracts* 25: 4012; January 1965.

339. S. EDWARD WEINSWIG. "Evaluation of Lessons To Teach Introductory Skills in Grade Four." Doctor's Dissertation, Boston University School of Education, 1962. *Dissertation Abstracts* 23: 1295; October 1962.

340. JOHN C. WEISER and JAMES E. HAYES. "Democratic Attitudes of Teachers and Prospective Teachers." *Phi Delta Kappan* 47: 476-81; May 1966.

341. SHIRLEY CAROLINE WENDT. "A Survey of the Educational Backgrounds and the Problems Met by a Selected Group of Elementary Teachers Teaching Social Studies in Homeroom in a Metropolitan Area." Doctor's Dissertation, Wayne State University, 1963. *Dissertation Abstracts* 25: 5702-5703; April 1965.

342. EDITH WEST. *Preparation and Evaluation of Social Studies Curriculum Guides and Materials for Grades K to 14.* USOE Project 5-0659. (ERIC ED 023 690) Minneapolis: University of Minnesota.

343. EDITH WEST. "University of Minnesota: an Articulated Curriculum for Grades K-14." *Social Education* 29: 209-11; April 1965.

344. A. F. WESTIN and RAYMOND E. SMITH. "Learning To Teach About Liberty: An Institute Model for the 1970's." *Social Education* 32: 355-61; April 1968.

345. RALPH LEE WHITE. "An Analysis of the Social Studies

Teacher Education Curriculum in Selected Tennessee Institutions." Doctor's Dissertation, The University of Tennessee, 1960. *Dissertation Abstracts* 21: 320; August 1960.

346. ROY C. WHITE. "A Study Associating Selected Conservation Understandings with Available Community Resources for Grades Four Through Twelve." Doctor's Dissertation, University of Montana, 1967. *Dissertation Abstracts* 28: 1638A; November 1967.

347. HENRY I. WILLETT, JR. "The Development and Testing of a Method of Textual Materials Selection." Doctor's Dissertation, University of Virginia, 1967. *Dissertation Abstracts* 28: 3448-49A; March 1968.

348. RICHARD L. WING. *The Production and Evaluation of Three Computer-Based Economics Games for the Sixth Grade.* USOE Project 5-0320. (ERIC ED 014 227) Yorktown Heights, Westchester County, New York: New York Department of Education.

349. ROBERT WILLIAM WOOD. "Basic Sociological Understandings Desirable for Inclusion in the Elementary School Social Studies Curriculum." Doctor's Dissertation, University of Montana, 1968. *Dissertation Abstracts* 29: 1178A-79A; October 1968.

350. SISTER M. STEPHANIE ZIMMER. "An Analysis of Map Skill Deficiencies in Elementary School Children." Doctor's Dissertation, The Catholic University of America, 1967. *Dissertation Abstracts* 28: 2107A; December 1967.

351. ROGER MARVIN ZIMMERMAN. "An Analysis of the Treatment of Famous Individuals in Six Elementary School Social Studies Textbook Series (Parts I and II)." Doctor's Dissertation, University of Minnesota, 1967. *Dissertation Abstracts* 28: 2468A; January 1968.